USING THE
CAS PROFESSIONAL STANDARDS

NASPA.
Student Affairs Administrators
in Higher Education

Council for the
Advancement of
Standards in Higher Education

ACPA
College Student
Educators International

USING THE
CAS PROFESSIONAL STANDARDS

Diverse Examples of Practice

EDITORS
Needham Yancey Gulley, Shannon R. Dean, and **Laura A. Dean**

Using the CAS Professional Standards: Diverse Examples of Practice

Copyright © 2017 by the National Association of Student Personnel Administrators (NASPA), Inc.; American College Personnel Association (ACPA); and the Council for the Advancement of Standards in Higher Education (CAS). All rights reserved.

Published by
NASPA–Student Affairs Administrators in Higher Education
111 K Street, NE
10th Floor
Washington, DC 20002

ACPA–College Student Educators International
One Dupont Circle, NW
Suite 300
Washington, DC 20036

Council for the Advancement of Standards in Higher Education
123 N. College Ave.
Suite 250
Fort Collins, CO 80524

Library of Congress Cataloging-in-Publication Data

Names: Gulley, Needham Yancey.
Title: Using the CAS professional standards : diverse examples of practice / Needham Yancey Gulley, Shannon R. Dean, and Laura A. Dean, Editors.
Description: Washington, DC : NASPA-Student Affairs Administrators in Higher Education, ACPA College Student Educators International, and Council for the Advancement of Standards in Higher Education, [2017] | Includes bibliographical references and index.
Identifiers: LCCN 2016054093 (print) | LCCN 2017001343 (ebook) | ISBN 9780931654701 (hardcover) | ISBN 9780931654695 (ePub) | ISBN 9780931654688 (Mobi)
Subjects: LCSH: Student affairs services--Standards--United States. | Universities and colleges--Standards--United States.
Classification: LCC LB2342.9 .G85 2017 (print) | LCC LB2342.9 (ebook) | DDC 371.4--dc23
LC record available at https://lccn.loc.gov/2016054093

Printed and bound in the United States of America

FIRST EDITION

Contents

Introduction   ix
Laura A. Dean

Chapter 1 **Overview of the CAS Professional Standards**   1
Marybeth Drechsler Sharp

Chapter 2 **Learning Outcomes in Program**   17
Evaluation and Assessment
Shannon R. Dean

Chapter 3 **General Use of the CAS Standards:**   27
A Vice President's Perspective
Tim James Pierson and Onie McKenzie

Chapter 4 **Using the CAS Standards for**   37
Divisionwide Program Review:
The Case of a Regional Institution
Mary-Jeanne Raleigh and John R. Jones III

Chapter 5 **Using the CAS Standards With a**   49
Whole Division: A Student Affairs
Assessment Officer's View
Jennifer Wells

Chapter 6 **Using the CAS Standards in Academic**   61
Advising: The Community College Setting
Adrian Rodriguez and Louann Schulze

Chapter 7 **Using the CAS Standards at a**   77
Multicampus Institution: The Arkansas
State University–Beebe Story
Deborah Garrett and David Mayes

Chapter 8 **Using the CAS Standards in Housing**   89
           and Residence Life: Lessons From
           a Small Private Institution
           Dave Rozeboom

Chapter 9 **Using the CAS Standards for LGBTQ**   105
           Services: Examples From a Large
           Public Research Institution
           Alex C. Lange

Chapter 10 **Adapting the CAS Framework: The Case**   119
           for Cross-Functional Standards
           Léna Kavaliauskas Crain

Chapter 11 **The CAS Approach: Diverse Examples,**   133
           Multiple Lessons
           Needham Yancey Gulley

Appendix A **CAS Self-Study: Roles,**   141
           Responsibilities, and Timeline

Appendix B **CAS Review Executive Summary**   145
           and Action Plan

Appendix C **Reference Sheet for Completing**   151
           Outcome Planning

Appendix D **Division of Student Affairs:**   155
           Directions for Planning and
           Assessment Worksheet

Appendix E **Department Annual Summary:**   159
           Student Affairs

Appendix F **CAS Student Learning and Development** 163
Domains and Dimensions

The Authors 165
Index 173

Introduction

Laura A. Dean

The standards, guidelines, and self-assessment guides published by the Council for the Advancement of Standards in Higher Education (CAS) have been available for decades, and they have attained broad acceptance by higher education practitioners, particularly in areas traditionally associated with student affairs. More than 40 professional associations choose to hold membership in CAS and to send representatives to engage in the work of standards development and promulgation; these organizations support the work of CAS by offering related professional development to their members and, in many cases, providing the relevant functional area standards on their websites. Still, one of the most frequently asked questions is about what using the CAS approach looks like in practice and how the CAS materials and philosophy can be implemented in various settings. It is for that reason that we developed this book. Although the editors are now faculty members teaching in student affairs/higher education preparation programs, all of us have had significant work experiences as practitioners, and we recognize the utility that the CAS standards and processes offer for local assessment projects. We also recognize the value in providing real-life examples that can inform practice for professionals in the field. For that reason, we invited practitioners to write chapters that reflect a wide range of institutional types, functional areas, perspectives, and uses of the CAS standards and processes. We hope that readers will find answers to their questions regarding the CAS approach and materials and useful examples to draw on for their work.

CAS is nearly 40 years old and in that time has created, published, and updated multiple standards and guidelines, self-assessment guides, learning and development outcomes, a statement of shared ethical principles, and a set of characteristics of individual excellence. Countless conference workshops and presentations, multiple book chapters, and several journal articles describe studies designed to assess levels of awareness of the CAS standards and the extent of their use by practitioners. However, what has been absent is a compilation of in-depth case studies that show what the CAS approach looks like in practice. That is the gap we seek to address in this book.

OUR APPROACH

We hold several assumptions, and they helped to frame this book. First, we are proponents of CAS, as are the chapter authors we invited to be a part of this project. We believe that the collaborative, consensus-oriented approach that CAS uses yields standards that represent the best thinking of a wide range of professionals and that reflect broad agreement about what constitutes good practice. We believe that standards of practice offer a useful touchstone for comparison of local practice to broader benchmarks. We believe that the CAS standards and guidelines are useful for program review but that CAS materials can inform practice in many other ways as well. Finally, we believe that the best way to help practitioners use the CAS approach most effectively is to offer examples from other practitioners who are doing the work—and doing it well.

The cover of the 9th edition of *CAS Professional Standards for Higher Education* (CAS, 2015) pictured aspen trees, which also appear on the cover of this companion book. As Jen Wells pointed out in her Editor's Note (CAS, 2015), aspens are known for their ability to thrive in a wide range of conditions. She likened their shared root system to the CAS standards, which collectively provide a solid foundation for our work and firm grounding across various and changing circumstances. The functional area standards are like the individual trees, with unique characteristics that distinguish them, yet joined by the common root system that connects them. The chapters in this book also reflect this idea. The CAS standards and approach serve as a common foundation, but their use looks different in practice across settings and situations.

The chapters here offer contextual information on CAS, including its history and scope, and on related topics, like learning and development outcomes, as well as chapters that describe the CAS standards in practice in a variety of settings. The book is generally divided into three segments: Chapters 1 and 2 are foundational, Chapters 3 through 10 represent various applications of the CAS approach and CAS materials, and Chapter 11 offers some thoughts about the larger picture and lessons learned.

A CLOSER LOOK

Chapter 1 is useful for both readers who are unfamiliar with CAS and those who use the standards but may not know, or may have forgotten, how they came about and the values and beliefs that underlie them. Marybeth Drechsler Sharp, executive director of CAS, offers a glimpse into the origins of CAS and provides an overview of the self-assessment–based program review process, which is the way the standards are most frequently used. This will be useful to readers who have questions about later chapters and need a refresher on the basic self-study process.

Chapter 2 focuses on student learning and development outcomes (SLDOs). Any department or unit needs to consider both its organizational processes and the effect its work has on the students it serves; the CAS standards reflect the importance of both. The ultimate goal of our work is student learning, growth, and success, and the SLDOs offer a framework for developing and assessing our effectiveness in this area. In this chapter, Shannon Dean gives an overview of learning and development outcomes and discusses their use as an integral element of comprehensive assessment.

Chapters that provide real-life examples of how the CAS standards are used comprise the core of this book. We intentionally invited authors who represent a range of institution types and sizes, functional areas, administrative positions and perspectives, and approaches to using the CAS standards. In Chapter 3, Tim Pierson and Onie McKenzie reflect on the divisional viewpoint of using the CAS standards for a long-standing divisionwide approach and describe the benefits that have resulted. Shifting from this description of an institution in which the CAS approach is well-established, Mary-Jeanne Raleigh and John Jones in Chapter 4 provide insight about how the CAS standards and program review process were introduced and integrated at a mid-size regional institution as a component of a new learning outcomes–focused strategic plan. The description of this approach to training staff will be particularly useful for readers who are considering how to introduce the CAS standards and process into their own settings. In Chapter 5, the last of the division-level chapters, Jen Wells offers her perspective as an assessment professional working to develop a culture of assessment in a student affairs division. Describing specific initiatives, she gives insight into how intentional and creative strategies can shift a division culture effectively, particularly at institutions that may be in transition.

CAS develops standards with the intent that they be applicable to all institution types and sizes, and the next two chapters examine the use of the standards in complex institutional structures. In Chapter 6, Adrian Rodriguez and Louann Schulze describe the complexities of using CAS for a comprehensive review of student services at a large, multicampus community college, in preparation for their regional accreditation reaffirmation process. Accreditation is often an impetus for program review, and the authors focus on the review of academic advising, including consideration of learning outcomes assessment. In Chapter 7, Deb Garrett and David Mayes offer another perspective on using the CAS standards at a smaller institution that also includes multiple campuses and delivery sites; particular attention is given to creating review teams that reflect organizational differences among locations. While these two chapters focus on the use of the CAS standards across multiple areas at complex institutions, Chapter 8 examines the use of the standards in a single functional area at small colleges. Smaller private institutions have different challenges and opportunities, and Dave Rozeboom describes in detail how the standards have been used productively in residence life programs at three different small to mid-size institutions.

Although the CAS standards are most often used for program review, the materials lend themselves to a number of other uses. In Chapter 9, Alex Lange discusses how the CAS standards are used to inform program development related to identifying learning outcomes, benchmarking against professional standards, and engaging in institutional advocacy. Written in the context of a lesbian, gay, bisexual, transgender, and queer resource center at a large public institution, the chapter describes the use of additional, area-specific professional standards to supplement the CAS standards, as well as considers the CAS standards from other areas whose functions overlap with those of the resource center.

CAS publishes standards and guidelines for more than 40 functional areas, but there are still many areas—or combinations of areas—for which standards do not exist. In any case, it is still possible to use the CAS standards in such situations, and in Chapter 10, the final chapter in this section, Léna Kavaliauskas Crain discusses how the standards were adapted to address the features of a unique program focused on the senior year at a large public institution.

Finally, in the concluding chapter, Yancey Gulley identifies some of the common lessons from the preceding chapters and reflects on successful strategies in developing a culture of evidence and assessment. He leaves us with reminders about good practice and questions to guide practitioners' use of the standards.

OUR HOPE

The CAS standards are more than meets the eye; rather than being simply an arbitrary set of expectations or aspirational "best practice" goals, they are descriptions of what good practice looks like—and they challenge practitioners to consider the relationship between inputs and outcomes in strategic ways. Additionally, these standards are grounded in theory, informed by research, and vetted by both experts and the broad perspectives of representatives from more than 40 professional associations across higher education. They were conceived of and developed to provide practitioners with the means to assess their programs and services effectively and reliably, and thus to ensure consistent and high-quality outcomes.

Similarly, this book was conceived and developed to provide readers with examples of what it looks like when the CAS approach is used, and used well. There are as many ways to apply the CAS approach as there are campuses that do so. While it is well beyond the scope of any book to represent the full picture, we wanted to recognize and illustrate the diversity that exists. We hope that you will read beyond the specific contexts and cases described to see the ideas and strategies reflected therein; for example, an approach used at a large, multicampus institution can offer lessons that are applicable at a small residential campus as well. As you read, we encourage you to look beyond the surface characteristics and consider what you can learn that might apply in your own setting or that sparks an idea for you.

There is no one "right" way to use the CAS standards or to do a CAS-based self-study, and we have not chosen the examples in this book because they are somehow correct or the "best" according to a defined metric. As the CAS standards are statements of good practice, we believe that these chapters are examples of good practice. They vary in approach, tone, and structure. The descriptions are not completely consistent in terms of what the authors did or how they did it—nor were they intended to be. However, they all reflect uses of the CAS approach and CAS standards that honor the integrity of the standards, adapt processes in intentional ways to fit local contexts and needs, and focus on maintaining high-quality programs and services that contribute to student success. We hope that they will encourage you to find new and more effective ways to incorporate the CAS standards into your work with creativity, care, and confidence.

REFERENCE

Council for the Advancement of Standards in Higher Education. (2015). *CAS professional standards for higher education* (9th ed.). Washington, DC: Author.

Chapter 1

Overview of the CAS Professional Standards

Marybeth Drechsler Sharp

Recently, higher education has been subject to increased scrutiny from lawmakers, employers, parents, journalists, and the public at large. Questions abound regarding how to know what students are learning, whether postsecondary education covers what society needs, why some students take longer than others to complete their degrees (if they complete them at all), and more. Ensuing conversations seek to identify responsibility for failings as well as solutions to perceived problems, and system-level difficulties are frequently attributed to limited funding, government mandates, and underprepared students. In one appraisal of how higher education must shift its practices to address challenges, Pennington (2012) asserted that "institutions should improve student success by focusing on practices within their control instead of blaming external factors" (para. 4). But which practices matter most, and how can we know?

In 1979, the Council for the Advancement of Standards in Higher Education (CAS) was founded for the purpose of crafting professional standards designed to guide quality higher education practice. The *CAS Professional Standards for Higher Education*, written and maintained by this consortium of higher education professional associations, are distinctively devised to help postsecondary institutions respond to aspects of the current push for accountability, given their emphasis on essential components of quality of student programs and services. Rooted in tested practices and relevant professional literature, the broadly agreed upon CAS standards can be helpful in designing critical programs and services, as well as assisting with the evaluation of those programs and services. CAS standards, dually oriented on program outcomes and student outcomes, empower professionals to make difficult decisions about where they must invest time, staffing, and resources. CAS standards guide educators and professionals as they develop and assess high-quality environments and structures that influence student learning, development, and success. This chapter will situate CAS within the broader landscape of the movement for higher education accountability, provide an introduction to the CAS organization and its philosophical underpinnings, explain the structure of the CAS standards, and offer recommendations for using CAS for self-regulation through program review.

ACCOUNTABILITY IN HIGHER EDUCATION

Through the cacophony of calls for accountability around postsecondary completion rates, workforce preparedness, and educational access, higher education is being challenged to verify that the structures in place help students to learn, grow, and succeed. According to Matthews, Zanville, and Duncan, internal and external constituents of higher education are asking, "Do our degrees, certificates, and other credentials stand for high quality? What is the learning—the skills— that our credentials signify? How do we know learning has occurred and that skills have been acquired?" (Lumina Foundation, 2016, p. 2). Educators are being asked to provide more direct evidence of student learning, and traditional mechanisms for evaluating and accrediting institutions are being questioned. In many cases, competencies, outcomes, badges, and credentials have been utilized as means of gathering increasingly relevant information about students' college experiences.

Opportunities for student learning, development, and success are not restricted to classroom environments in postsecondary higher education. "Research informs us that integrated, interdisciplinary learning requires faculty to move beyond a discipline-based orientation to work with educators across the institution and practitioners in the employer world" (Lumina Foundation, 2016, p. 3), and professionals working in student programs and services must reach out to their academic colleagues with ideas for cross-functional and cocurricular collaboration. The programs and services addressed through the CAS standards, for example, provide necessary support structures, environments, and opportunities that enhance student success. Professionals across postsecondary education must implement intentional high-quality practices, measure the associated outcomes for student participants, and span traditional academic and student affairs boundaries to contribute to desired outcomes for students. "We need to build common cause among communities of practice (faculty, courageous leaders) who can change the belief system in higher education, and to convince faculty, administrators, and trustees that it is everyone's job to improve every student's success" (Pennington, 2012, para. 20). From the CAS perspective, student learning, development, and success are influenced holistically across higher education settings; the entirety of educational experiences for students requires intentionality and accountability.

INCEPTION AND GROWTH OF CAS

The history of CAS is rooted in the growth of the student affairs profession and in movements for greater accountability across higher education. In the 1960s, several associations collaborated to devise a professionwide entity that could speak as a resonant voice for student services. Ten student affairs associations endeavored to establish a group called the Council of Student Personnel Associations in Higher Education (COSPA), and in the late 1960s, the consortium published a well-regarded and progressive statement by its Commission of Professional Development titled "Student Development Services in Post-Secondary Education" (Cooper, 1975). COSPA was dissolved in 1976, in part due to association politics.

Several years after COSPA's dissolution, CAS was established to help the student services profession define and encourage high-quality preparation and practice. At the time CAS was being formed, several national associations were working to develop accreditation standards for academic programs that prepare counselors and counselor educators; that effort resulted in the creation of the Council for the Accreditation of Counseling and Related Educational Programs (CACREP). CACREP's focus on standards for educational preparation motivated the American College Personnel Association (ACPA) to consider devising standards to guide master's-level college student affairs administration programs, and ACPA invited the National Association of Student Personnel Administrators (NASPA) to collaborate. These two comprehensive student affairs associations convened a joint exploratory meeting of representatives from their own memberships, as well as delegates from seven other student affairs–oriented organizations, in June 1979. A second meeting in September 1979 resulted in the development of CAS as a nonprofit consortium with 11 charter member associations, collectively oriented on developing and disseminating professional standards designed to be used for self-assessment, rather than accreditation, in order to guide student affairs practice and academic preparation of student programs and services professionals. The acronym "CAS" stood for the Council for the Advancement of Standards for Student Services/Development Programs.

Although similar in structure to COSPA, CAS adopted a more narrow focus on common values, specifically pertaining to standards for and assessment of professional practice. In 1992, CAS was renamed the Council for the Advancement of Standards in Higher Education to reflect an expanded context for the council's higher education focus. Today, CAS member associations share the vision of "setting the standard for quality in higher education" and collaborate through processes necessary for accomplishing this vision and corresponding mission.

The landscape of higher education and the work of educators in student programs and services have changed, and CAS continues to adapt to represent the field and meet the needs of its constituents. Today, CAS boasts 43 member associations based within the United States and Canada and represents more than 115,000 higher education professionals and service providers. The book of standards, *CAS Professional Standards for Higher Education*, is in its ninth edition. The first 16 CAS standards were published with the support of the American College Testing Program in 1986; today, CAS has generated more than 40 sets of functional area standards and guidelines as well as a set of master's-level academic program standards for student affairs preparation. Also, CAS has formulated resources to promote individual excellence for professionals in higher education; articulate ethical principles, held in common across the many areas of professional practice represented at CAS; and model learning and development outcomes, intended to yield quality outcomes. In its nearly four decades of existence, CAS has facilitated the development of professionwide criteria and standards for quality practice through its collaborative work on behalf of higher education professionals who believe the learning, development, and success of all students to be the essence of higher education.

At its inception and in its early years, CAS was largely comprised of professional associations representing traditional student services functions, including housing, career services, orientation, student unions, and campus activities. Over time, the need for an expanded scope became evident, and new voices emerged at the CAS table to speak on behalf of such functional areas as developmental education, learning centers, academic advising, honors colleges, health centers, college stores, and testing centers.

Each member association designates one or two individuals to serve as representatives to CAS on behalf of its membership. These association representatives comprise the CAS Board of Directors, and collectively they are responsible for the preparation, revision, and approval of the CAS standards. Using a consensus approach to writing standards for functional areas, CAS representatives form committees to initially draft new standards or revise existing standards. Through a rigorous process, designated committees engage experts from around the field to provide insight, consult current research, incorporate established high-quality practices into the standards, and vet final standards drafts for the approval of the complete cadre of CAS representatives.

THE CAS PHILOSOPHY

The core beliefs underlying and informing CAS's work derive from theories and concepts germane to human development, student learning, group dynamics, organizational management, and administration. The guiding principles for CAS, which mirror those that inform the work of higher education professionals, can broadly be organized into the following five categories.

1. **Students and Their Environments:** Intentionally created educational environments that reflect a diverse society provide

opportunities for students to learn and grow. Within these settings, students should be perceived holistically, treated individually, and empowered with responsibility for their learning.

2. **Diversity and Multiculturalism:** CAS values diversity and
    multiculturalism; the standards advocate that professionals
    embrace diversity and eliminate barriers to create socially just,
    respectful communities. "The CAS standards reinforce that
    those responsible for creating educational environments need to
    be open to and accepting of differences, and they must recognize
    that such environments are important for enhancing the quality
    of the education provided and the learning achieved" (CAS,
    2015, pp. 3–4).

3. **Organization, Leadership, and Human Resources:** Each
    postsecondary institution is unique, and the specific missions
    and intended outcomes of programs and services should shape
    its structures and direct its efforts. Successful programs and
    services require leadership, and individuals providing direction
    should be experienced, knowledgeable, and well qualified.

4. **Health-Engendering Environments:** Students learn and
    develop in postsecondary environments that provide an appro-
    priate balance of challenge and support in and out of the class-
    room. Appropriate facilities, staffing, and finances complement
    quality programming, educational interventions, and learn-
    ing opportunities.

5. **Ethical Considerations:** Postsecondary educators must adhere
    to ethical standards in both their professional and personal lives
    to ensure fair and equitable practice in work with students and
    with one another.

The aforementioned guiding principles are evidenced in the construction and content of the standards written by the CAS consortium,

as well as through the approaches CAS takes to developing tools that accompany the standards and to promulgating resources.

WHAT ARE THE CAS STANDARDS?

The array of student programs and services addressed through the CAS standards share a common framework, called the General Standards. Although the specialized nature of functional areas is important to capture in the standards, CAS deems it essential to emphasize the similarities. For example, all programs and services need to have mission statements that align with the institution's mission, fair and equitable hiring practices, and guiding codes of ethics. In spite of the differences between functions, CAS identifies 12 sections of standards that programs and standards share.

These common criteria are relevant for every functional area, regardless of primary purpose, and thus, the General Standards form the core for nearly all CAS standards—even appearing verbatim, embedded within each set. The subsections of the General Standards include mission; program; organization and leadership; human resources; ethics; law, policy, and governance; diversity, equity, and access; internal and external relations; financial resources; technology; facilities and equipment; and assessment. Within the standards, statements have been crafted broadly to encompass all of the distinctive functional responsibilities that may exist at various types of institutions, while simultaneously providing specific enough information to offer useful direction. Reviewed and revised on a 3-year cycle, the CAS General Standards are timely, relevant, and responsive to changes within higher education.

A primary benefit of the General Standards is the boundary-spanning nature of their design. In many postsecondary institutions, professionals' responsibilities are divided into administrative entities and separated from other units. The effect of having many individual departments can be likened to siloes. In each silo, individuals have roles and responsibilities that appear unique; yet, elsewhere on campus other units are completing similar tasks, working toward comparable goals, and sometimes devising processes that are not consistent between siloes. Students experience higher education in far more seamless ways than our organizations are designed, and the functional area siloes belie those experiences. The effect of such siloed functional areas is isolating for faculty and staff, in addition to baffling students.

The General Standards shed light on the opportunities for connection among autonomous units. "The General Standards make the CAS standards highly utilitarian and promote inter-departmental, inter-program, and inter-service cooperation and collaboration" (CAS, 2015, p. 11). Professionals seeking connection between administrative units can use the General Standards to illustrate commonalities over differences. The General Standards may also prove helpful to offices or units for which functional area standards do not exist, since they offer a framework and standards that are applicable across all areas. Additionally, offices that contain numerous functional area responsibilities (e.g., student leadership, campus activities, civic engagement) may choose to start an assessment with the General Standards. "Since the General Standards are present in each set of standards, practitioners can identify both points of overlap and portions that speak to the various functions, enabling them to merge the General Standards and specialized aspects into one non-repetitive set of standards that reflects the complex nature of the office" (CAS, 2015, p. 11). The General Standards have appeared in each CAS publication, and they are continually evolving with the field of higher education. By including common standards across the functional areas, CAS has emphasized their widespread importance and the value of identifying similarities within and across institutions.

SELF-REGULATION USING THE CAS STANDARDS

By design, the CAS standards are intended for self-regulatory purposes rather than credentialing, certifying, or accrediting programs and services. According to Wheelan and Elgart (2016), "Self-regulation and respect for the uniqueness of institutions is a reason that American higher education continues to be the best, most diverse system in the world" (para. 12). Individual institutions, programs, and services ideally should direct their own assessments of quality and effectiveness. Because professionals working within a program or service most clearly understand its mission, goals, capacity, and resources, their expertise is preferred for CAS self-assessment processes over external review or regulation.

The CAS initiative emerged at a time when obtaining accreditation for academic programs was very desirable for institutions; in several ways, early CAS materials were modeled on standards and criteria devised by regional agencies. "Setting standards and evaluating their use on campus, engaging institutions in the reflective process of self-study, and using expert and peer review to promote continuous improvement are activities that accrediting agencies have been conducting and refining for more than 100 years" (Wheelan & Elgart, 2016, para. 12). Although assessment and evaluation in higher education have changed over the course of CAS's existence, the influence of accreditors on the CAS model of program review remains evident. Adopting the CAS standards for self-assessment is a means of benchmarking programs and services against widely accepted professional criteria.

A self-regulatory approach is concentrated on developing, sustaining, and enriching high-quality programs and services. CAS materials may be useful for supporting accreditation processes by providing evidence of cocurricular assessment and benchmarking against professional standards. "Programs and services committed to self-regulation continually assess their work, identify areas for improvement, and address those needs to maintain high quality programs and services" (CAS, 2015, p. 5). However CAS materials are used, efforts should be motivated from within and be oriented on continuous improvement.

CAS SELF-ASSESSMENT

A methodical and rigorous means of evaluating the quality of a program or service is to benchmark against the nationally accepted CAS standards through a program review process. To assist professionals with this self-study of their work, CAS recommends a seven-step approach. With the aid of the CAS Self-Assessment Guides (SAGs), professionals can thoroughly review their programs and services, compare evidence of their program's quality to established standards, and identify areas for further improvement.

Plan the Process

Before beginning a program review self-study, professionals must identify the area (or areas) to be evaluated and the rationale for the project. For example, institutional leaders planning for reaccreditation may decide to review individual programs and services; other motives for embarking on a self-study could arise because of program goals or needs. Regardless of reasoning, professionals will want to articulate expected outcomes and identify who will receive the results to help them design their review process. In preparing for the program review, individuals should devise a realistic process timeline, lay out their steps in the process, and work with other program or service staff members on the planning. By involving colleagues and stakeholders in the early phases of a program review, professionals can garner support and investment in the evaluation process and its results.

Assemble and Educate the Self-Assessment Team

Through the planning stage, professionals will begin to identify who should serve as program review team members based on the intended outcomes and audience for the review. A functional area program review typically includes three to five team members, one of whom should be a knowledgeable individual from outside the area under review. In the case of a large department or unusually complex department review, seven or eight individuals may comprise the team—this distributes the workload without reducing the team's pace. CAS recommends that the positional leader of the unit under review not serve as its chair. Placing another leader in the chair role can lend credibility, as well as help to ensure openness and honesty.

After assembling the program review team, professionals must train the members on foundational information about CAS standards and self-assessment. The team will need to review the CAS functional area standard(s) being used for the self-study and ensure that all members have similar understanding of the statements. Through training and dialogue, the team members should discuss their different interpretations of standards, establish ground rules for their work together, and determine how they will achieve consensus on their ratings and judgments. Finally, in this preliminary step of building a review team, members should examine the guidelines that accompany CAS standards to decide if they will include any of them in their review as a way of evaluating practice that goes beyond the threshold of the standards.

Identify, Collect, and Review Evidence

An essential component of any self-study is collecting evidence and documentation to support the review team's evaluations of program effectiveness. Team members should gather relevant information to support their program's efforts regularly; a review team can use the existing documents as a foundation and then collect additional information as needed. Each section of a SAG offers recommendations for documentary evidence to collect before rating program elements; examples of evidence to compile include student recruitment and marketing materials, program and administrative documents, assessment and evaluation data, staff reports, and data on cocurricular student engagement. The evidence gathered for a self-study will help the team assess a program's quality using the SAG criteria, and members can judge a program against the standards using multiple forms of evidence.

Conduct and Interpret Ratings Using Evaluative Evidence

The program review team should review the documentary evidence and assign ratings to each individual criterion. The SAG provides a 4-point scale for rating the extent to which a practice of a program or service is in compliance with the standards. One tested approach is for each team member to rate items based on his or her interpretation of the data, and then for the group to collectively discuss and agree on final ratings. In the space provided for Rationale, the team should then explain its reasoning and describe what evidence contributed to the ratings assigned within each subsection. Using the collective ratings, review team members then interpret the results of the self-study, resolve lingering disagreements through additional data collection or dialogue, and discuss the summary overview questions that conclude each subsection of the SAG. The review team should meet with the staff, students, and stakeholders from the program or service to share results from the self-study, as appropriate within institutional processes.

Develop an Action Plan

Drafting an action plan should begin with the review team's assessment of the program's strengths and weaknesses as compared to the CAS standards. To identify areas for improvement, team members should review items rated as Insufficient Evidence/Unable to Rate, Does Not Meet, or Partly Meets, and identify instances where raters disagreed. An action plan should include identified discrepancies, corrective actions, and recommended steps. When the team finds discrepancies between the standard statements and program practice, they can recommend improvements or adjustments to existing operations. Suggestions for corrective action should subdivide large tasks into smaller pieces, to enable the program or service to take reasonable steps toward achieving its desired quality. A review team should recommend specific action steps, prioritize these actions according to importance and needs, and outline the resources needed. The corrective action plan should also include an implementation time frame and benchmarks for accomplishment. Some institutions choose to have this part of the process done by staff from the functional area studied, rather than the review team, so that their knowledge of the area can inform the action plan and their involvement in its creation can increase their buy-in. To bring closure to a self-study process, functional area staff members should identify and establish priorities for the program based on its results and desired outcomes. The action plan devised after the program review should develop strategies for both building on program strength and tackling areas for improvement.

Prepare a Report

A self-study process should be recorded in a final report summarizing the program's mission, purpose, and philosophy; describing the program review process; explaining the self-assessment results; and delineating action plans. Reports may also explain how evidence was gathered and ratings assigned. The action plan for improving a program should be clearly articulated through the report, including necessary resources, a timeline for implementation, and responsible parties. Finally, drafting an executive summary or short presentation about the self-assessment can be helpful for program leaders who need to disseminate results and action plans to stakeholders and divisional leadership.

Close the Loop

The final step of a successful self-assessment process requires that the staff, students, and colleagues put the results into practice to enhance the quality of their program or service. To close the loop, the program leaders and stakeholders will need to navigate political hurdles, garner resources, dismantle barriers, and gain support for the next steps. To enact the recommendations of the action plan, program staff and leaders should discuss self-assessment results routinely—at staff meetings, during trainings, and in supervision—to make reflection and evaluation on program quality an ongoing aspect of the work and culture.

EMPLOYING THE CAS STANDARDS

Members of the higher education community find the CAS standards useful for numerous tasks in their professional roles. Intended to help professionals enhance their practice, the standards aggregate quality approaches and key components of student programs and services. CAS makes recommendations for several ways to use the standards, but the consortium stops short of being overly prescriptive. The flexibility of CAS materials is an asset of the tools, and professionals are able to adapt or customize aspects of the self-assessment instruments to fit their institution, program, services, or functional responsibilities. CAS advises that, in program review, professionals limit modifications to the standards statements; it discourages arbitrarily picking and choosing which standards to follow or disregard, since the standards are intended to reflect the threshold essentials of good practice. In certain circumstances, however, particular standards may not apply to a program or service (because the function resides in a different office at the particular institution, for example), or professionals may find it helpful to incorporate CAS guidelines or relevant standards from other professional associations into their self-study.

Professionals routinely use CAS standards to design new programs and services, gauge the effectiveness of programs, assess programs and services as part of accreditation self-studies, and shape staff development curricula. The CAS Learning and Development Outcome Domains and Dimensions assist programs and services with identifying related outcomes for their endeavors. The process of completing a CAS self-assessment for program review can assist professionals who must make difficult decisions about resource allocation, staffing capacity, and designing environments that respond to student needs.

Through the following chapters, individuals engaged within different programs, divisions, and institutions describe the approaches their units have taken to designing programs and services, developing student learning and development outcomes, and assessing the quality of their work. These examples are real-world cases in which professionals have used the CAS standards and self-study tools to understand and enhance their programs and services, and the stories will shed light on the ways others can employ these resources in their own settings.

REFERENCES

Cooper, A. C. (1975). Student development services in post-secondary education. *Journal of College Student Personnel, 16*(6), 524–528.

Council for the Advancement of Standards in Higher Education. (2015). *CAS professional standards for higher education* (9th ed.). Washington, DC: Author.

Lumina Foundation. (2016, June). *The emerging learning system: Report on the recent convening and new directions for action*. Indianapolis, IN: Author.

Pennington, H. (2012, April 8). For student success, stop debating and start improving. *The Chronicle of Higher Education*. Retrieved from http://chronicle.com/article/For-Student-Success-Stop/131451

Wheelan, B. S., & Elgart, M. A. (2016, May 25). Let accreditors do what does the most good for students. *The Chronicle of Higher Education*. Retrieved from http://chronicle.com/article/Let-Accreditors-Do-What-Does/236594

Chapter 2

Learning Outcomes in Program Evaluation and Assessment

Shannon R. Dean

earning outcomes define the goals of learning experiences (Keeling, Wall, Underhile, & Dungy, 2008) and are important in helping determine whether programs, courses, or functional areas are meeting the desired results. Learning outcomes have been an important part of my work as both a practitioner and now as a faculty member. As a practitioner, I developed outcomes that were associated with my various roles in housing and residence life; as the director for international student life, I developed departmental and programmatic outcomes in order to guide programming efforts and to assess student development. By starting at the desired end result—what I wanted students to learn—I could structure programs and services to focus on student learning; this approach also allowed better assessment of my intended student outcomes. Now, as a faculty member, I establish student learning outcomes as part of each course I teach, and I work with students as they develop their own sets of outcomes as part of an assessment and evaluation course in a student affairs in higher education program.

This chapter addresses the purpose and importance of learning outcomes and the challenges associated with implementing them. Recommendations for how to develop and use them in relationship to the CAS standards will also be addressed.

IMPORTANCE OF LEARNING OUTCOMES

Developing intended learning outcomes can be time-consuming and sometimes daunting, yet they are an important and vital element for guiding program development as well as for evaluating programs. Learning outcomes are critically important—they specify what students should learn, do, or demonstrate as a result of their participation in an experience (Bresciani, Zelna, & Anderson, 2004). There are internal and external reasons that student affairs professionals should be competent in understanding and utilizing them as part of program evaluation. Accountability, program improvement, student learning and development, and program or departmental effectiveness are some of the reasons for the increased need to demonstrate learning on college campuses.

Enrollment in colleges and universities across the United States grew in the post–World War II period, in the 1960s, and in the 1980s; along with this growth came greater scrutiny for higher education, as many called for more accountability in the 1990s and 2000s (Wingspread Group on Higher Education, 1993). Higher education and national student affairs organizations encouraged student affairs divisions to continue aligning their practices with the educational missions of their institutions (ACPA–College Student Educators International, 1996; American Association for Higher Education, ACPA, & NASPA–Student Affairs Administrators in Higher Education, 1998) and to assess their own contributions to these missions (Upcraft & Schuh, 1996). With calls for greater accountability in higher education, student affairs also underwent increased examination. Higher education and student affairs began to focus on ways to demonstrate student outcomes in relation to learning and development (Schuh, 2009). More than 20 years later the pressure for accountability for funds and student learning remains. Even today, colleges and universities are being held accountable for student completion rates and assessing intended learning outcomes is one way to demonstrate the gains associated with our programs and services while students work toward degree completion.

Besides accountability, another important reason to develop and assess learning outcomes is the value added as part of the assessment cycle (Schuh, 2009). This cycle, at a basic level, begins with administrators identifying the mission and goals of a program or office. Sometimes these goals are already in place and other times they need to be created. The next step is to identify what students should gain as a result of participation (intended objectives and outcomes) in the services and programs provided by the program or office—objectives are relatively broad, but outcomes are more specific in nature. After determining the intended outcomes, it is important to create and implement methods to achieve them. Next, it is necessary to gather evidence to determine the effectiveness of the program or method. This evidence can be collected in a number of ways, including but not limited to surveys, interviews, focus groups, and rubrics. Interpret the evidence and then make changes, if needed, based on the actual outcomes. These changes also aid in creating new intended outcomes, and thus the cycle begins again. Therefore, the development and use of intended outcomes is an essential component of the assessment cycle.

LEARNING OUTCOMES AND OBJECTIVES

There are often challenges in distinguishing between outcomes and objectives, and relating those specifically to the CAS standards. Objectives, sometimes described as goals, are the broad overarching purposes describing the intentions and values of a program or service. These are often focused on the program or facilitator. Outcomes, however, are specific and describe the end result and focus on the participants, typically students. Learning outcomes should be measurable, meaningful, and manageable.

Part of developing learning outcomes is writing them in a measurable way—this can often be the most difficult portion of development and will be discussed in more detail later in the chapter—but it is also important to ensure that the outcome is meaningful and manageable. For example, it may be meaningful for you to interview all student leaders in order for them to articulate their philosophies of leadership and what they are learning through their positions; however, if you have more than 100 student leaders and only a handful of staff members, it may not be a manageable outcome to assess. One way to ensure meaningful outcomes is to align them with the CAS standards. Remembering to make outcomes measurable, meaningful, and manageable is an important part of developing effective learning outcomes (Bresciani et al., 2004).

CAS LEARNING AND DEVELOPMENT OUTCOMES

There are 12 sections in the CAS General Standards (see Chapter 1) with common criteria regardless of functional area categories. Part two of the CAS standards refers to programs and identifies expectations that programs and services must contribute to student learning and development. As part of the program criteria in 2003, CAS identified 16 domains for student learning and development. These 16 domains were consolidated in 2008 into six domains: knowledge acquisition, construction, integration, and application; cognitive complexity; intrapersonal development; interpersonal competence; humanitarianism and civic engagement; and practical competence

(CAS, 2015; see Appendix F). Within each of these domains, CAS developed several learning outcome dimensions to aid in program development and assessment (CAS, 2015). For example, within the interpersonal competence domain, the dimensions include meaningful relationships, interdependence, collaboration, and effective leadership. Knowledge of these CAS standards and domains can aid professionals in creating effective and meaningful learning outcomes for their programs and services.

CHALLENGES

Student affairs professionals often face many challenges when developing learning outcomes. For example, writing them can be time-consuming. There are challenges often associated with the assessment process, the multiple iterations of learning outcomes, and the precision of writing measurable outcomes. Additionally, some individuals may feel that the purpose of learning outcomes is irrelevant to their work; others may resist the process of developing and assessing learning outcomes. These challenges, although seemingly overwhelming, can be reduced through effective training.

Although writing learning outcomes can indeed be time-consuming, effective training for student affairs practitioners can expedite the process. Student affairs professionals should feel competent in both writing and assessing outcomes associated with their programs and departments. Gaining comfortability with writing intended outcomes begins by asking ourselves what we want students to know or do as a result of our programs and services. When practitioners become comfortable with these thoughts, articulating learning in terms of outcomes begins to come more naturally. Thus, training practitioners in the importance and basics of writing good outcomes is helpful in getting practitioners to feel more competent. As part of the training process for writing them, practitioners should also understand how this practice (writing outcomes) is explicitly connected to assessing the outcomes. Many practitioners feel overwhelmed at the mere thought of assessment, but understanding its importance and making it manageable can help to alleviate some of the anxiety.

Some professionals may even question the validity of writing learning outcomes; but they are not only helpful in assessment, but also in the development and design of programs. By starting at the end—that is, what we want students to learn—we can purposely structure programs and services to focus on student learning. Although some practitioners may resist developing learning outcomes, this is crucial to creating intentional practices and providing evidence for student learning and development that occurs as a result of student affairs programs and departments.

WRITING INTENDED LEARNING OUTCOMES

As accountability continues to increase in higher education—and as student affairs stays committed to student learning and development—the need for program and departmental learning outcomes will also remain. Thus, student affairs professionals need to be competent in writing learning outcomes and understanding their benefits (ACPA, 2006; ACPA & NASPA, 2015). This section discusses how to write good learning outcomes; the benefits of outcome-based assessment; and how to advocate for the use of learning outcomes in program evaluation and assessment.

There are a few things to remember when writing learning outcomes. As previously noted, making sure the outcomes are meaningful, measurable, and manageable is crucial (Bresciani et al., 2004). Yet making sure they are measurable is one of the most difficult aspects of writing them (Schuh, 2009). Measurable outcomes identify a clear participant or audience for the desired outcome—often in programmatic outcomes, the participant will be the specific student for which the program is intended. Next, it is important to identify the desired behavior. Behaviors are expressed as verbs. For example, students will be able to articulate or demonstrate, determine or compare. Because learning is not a passive process, neither is the practice of demonstrating that learning or growth has occurred. The list of possible behaviors is extensive and truly depends on what you hope students gain as a result of a program. Bloom's (1984) taxonomy of learning domains and Fink's (2013) taxonomy of significant learning may be helpful in identifying desired behaviors and outcomes. Further, it is essential to determine the conditions for the outcome. For example, if students will be participating in a leadership development program, then that becomes the condition. Finally, it is key to determine the degree of measurement for your outcome; this can be very specific or more general. It is imperative that there is a plan in place for the measurement of the outcome, as part of the cycle of assessment discussed earlier. The following learning outcomes represent a more specific and a more general example of degrees in the outcome.

> *As a result of participating in resident assistant (RA) training, RAs will be able to demonstrate the procedures for documenting an incident, by filling out a mock incident report.*

> *As a result of participating in international student orientation, students will identify two offices on campus that provide academic support services for students.*

The first example provides a more specific degree of competency or effectiveness. Students will fill out a mock incident report to demonstrate that they have learned how to document incidents. The second example, however, is broader, and not readily measured one specific way—students could select two offices that provide academic support from a list, they could write in two offices as part of a program assessment, or they could be asked to identify these offices in a myriad of other ways. Regardless of how you go about assessing this, it is important to understand the method by which you will measure the learning outcome.

Collaborating with colleagues in your department is also beneficial in the development of strong learning outcomes. By asking for input into the process of program and departmental learning outcome development, you can help foster intentional practices and programs focused on learning outcomes. Furthermore, collaborative efforts help to ensure buy-in to the program, the intended learning outcome(s), and ultimately the assessment efforts to measure learning.

Another suggestion for writing effective learning outcomes is to solicit feedback from others. Many individuals and sometimes even specific offices exist on campuses that have assessment and outcomes as their area of specialization. Use these individuals to help construct your outcomes, or collaborate with other colleagues who feel competent in this area. Collaboration can produce the most intentional and effective learning outcomes for your office and programs.

By using learning outcomes as part of programs and departmental initiatives, professionals can provide data to administrators and others, thus better advocating for their departments. Evidence-based practice allows professionals to demonstrate the benefits of their offices, programs, and events. At a time when accountability is high, funds fewer, and resources slim, it is imperative to have evidence that attests to the necessity of our work and its impact on student learning and development.

REFERENCES

American Association for Higher Education, ACPA–College Student Educators International, & NASPA–Student Affairs Administrators in Higher Education. (1998). *Powerful partnerships: A shared responsibility for learning.* Washington, DC: Authors.

ACPA–College Student Educators International. (1996). The student learning imperative: Implications for student affairs. *Journal of College Student Development, 37*(2), 188–222.

ACPA–College Student Educators International. (2006). *ASK standards: Assessment skills and knowledge content standards for student affairs practitioners and scholars.* Washington, DC: Author.

ACPA–College Student Educators International & NASPA–Student Affairs Administrators in Higher Education. (2015). *Professional competency areas for student affairs educators.* Retrieved from http://www.naspa.org/images/uploads/main/ACPA_NASPA_Professional_Competencies_FINAL.pdf

Bloom, B. S. (1984). *Taxonomy of educational objectives.* New York, NY: Pearson Education.

Bresciani, M. J., Zelna, C. L., & Anderson, J. A. (2004). *Assessing student learning and development: A handbook for practitioners.* Washington, DC: National Association of Student Personnel Administrators.

Council for the Advancement of Standards in Higher Education. (2015). *CAS professional standards for higher education* (9th ed.). Washington, DC: Author.

Fink, D. (2013). *Creating significant learning experiences.* San Fancisco, CA: Jossey-Bass.

Keeling, R., Wall, A., Underhile, R., & Dungy, G. (2008). *Assessment reconsidered: Institutional effectiveness for student success.* Washington, DC: National Association of Student Personnel Administrators.

Schuh, J. H. (Ed.). (2009). *Assessment methods for student affairs.* San Francisco, CA: Jossey-Bass.

Upcraft, M. L., & Schuh, J. H. (1996). *Assessment in student affairs: A guide for practitioners.* San Francisco, CA: Jossey-Bass.

Wingspread Group on Higher Education. (1993). *An American imperative: Higher expectations for higher education.* Racine, WI: The Johnson Foundation.

Chapter 3

General Use of the CAS Standards
A Vice President's Perspective

Tim James Pierson and Onie McKenzie

The use of the Council for the Advancement of Standards in Higher Education (CAS) materials at Longwood University is deeply embedded in the fabric of student affairs. The late Phyllis Mable— founder, past president, and first executive director of CAS—served as Longwood's vice president for student affairs (VPSA) during the early stages of the standards' development. As Longwood's dean of students in the mid-1990s, Tim Pierson worked closely with Mable in the adoption of the CAS standards, and he continued to emphasize their application throughout the division when he succeeded her as vice president. Thus, the CAS standards have been an integral part of Longwood's assessment program for approximately 25 years. This chapter focuses on the multiple benefits gained through a sustained, long-term application of the standards across all departments/program areas within student affairs.

THE IMPORTANCE OF LEADERSHIP

One of the first lessons effective leaders learn is that well-defined priorities must be established in concert with the institution's mission and strategic plan. Furthermore, this conceptual alignment must be supported with sufficient financial resources and competent personnel. There is a reason successful sports teams invest in key positions—they will deliver, and not every player is good in every role! Onie McKenzie, Longwood's assistant vice president for student affairs (AVP) and coauthor of this chapter, has past experience both as a student affairs practitioner and in directing outcomes assessment from the academic provost's office. Consequently, she is the lead assessment administrator for Longwood's student affairs division and the subject matter expert in the successful implementation of the standards today. McKenzie has developed a program review process that is relevant and meaningful to the context of Longwood, and its cornerstone is the CAS standards. It is the vice president's responsibility to determine the best use of available resources that will have the most impact across the entire division, based on these reviews; allocating resources often requires making tough decisions, and making those decisions with the knowledge of professional standards and expectations is most beneficial. Thus, identifying and designating a position with primary responsibility as the division's lead assessment person is a prerequisite step in developing an effective team.

CAS self-studies, along with supporting documents that attest to departmental contribution to learning outcomes, serve as an excellent remedy for the chronic concern voiced by those student affairs professionals who feel less-than-equal to their academic affairs colleagues. Herein lies an opportunity for the astute student affairs leader to make a difference when formulating a strategic plan to change institutional norms that hinder student learning. In this age of increased accreditation accountability, using professional standards, guidelines, and competencies for guiding and evaluating the work of professional staff, programs, and services is essential, regardless of institutional type, staffing size, and funding.

SPECIFIC RECOMMENDATIONS FOR USING THE CAS STANDARDS

Each functional area within student affairs at Longwood University participates in a formal program review once every 5 years. As a result, three to four departments are involved in a yearlong review process annually within a widely publicized, predetermined rotation. With a twofold expectation, the review must be based on professional standards that are externally defined, and the assessment team should include stakeholders who are external to the departmental staff. A few departments (e.g., counseling and psychological services, police/public safety) have chosen to pursue professional accreditation that meets both review expectations. Given the history of success at Longwood and the perception of CAS as the continuing preeminent force for integrating standards into the assessment of higher education's programs, services, and student learning outcomes, most directors opt to participate in a self-study using the most recently published and relevant CAS Self-Assessment Guides (SAGs).

The AVP, with input from the student affairs program review team, provides both leadership and support to the program review process. The team is convened by the AVP and includes self-selected/supervisor-appointed representatives from all departments across the division. This team serves as a conduit between and among the VPSA, AVP, and the student affairs staff as a whole; it is also the means by which input into key assessment-related decisions is solicited and information and expectations shared. The team typically meets twice a month, and assessment-related education and training often constitute agenda items. Considered critically important to the success of the review process, all of the various CAS self-study materials and documents have been vetted by the assessment team and customized to streamline the

process while maintaining the integrity and intent of the CAS standards and SAGs. Examples of this customization follow.

To provide administrative support and accountability to the process,
the AVP: (a) meets regularly with self-study coordinators prior to the
review to ensure adequate preparation; (b) after extended mutual consultation with the self-study coordinators, issues a formal invitation
to each assessment team member; (c) coordinates and facilitates an
opening orientation meeting; (d) calculates collective average criterion and component ratings, based on individual ratings, and prepares
summary tables; and (e) consolidates all of the ratings as well as the
rationale notes/comments and responses to the overview questions
into a single document. Furthermore, the AVP collects and provides
documentary evidence for several of the 12 component areas when
the policies and procedures for an area are dictated at the institutional,
rather than the departmental, level. This allows the self-study coordinator to focus on collecting only the information that is unique to his or
her department, lessening the burden of providing all essential documentary evidence to the reviewers.

Because the CAS standards and SAGs are provided as guides to self-
assessment, revisions to the review process itself have been made with
input from the student affairs staff on the assessment team. Some of the
recommended CAS summary/planning worksheets have been eliminated.
Although the intent of the CAS component overview questions within
the SAGs is maintained, some questions deemed irrelevant or not
applicable to Longwood's institutional context were omitted; others were
consolidated to streamline the request for information. Reasons vary—
sometimes the expectation addressed by the question is something over
which departments at Longwood have no control or influence; as a state
agency, many practices regarding personnel are dictated at the institutional
level, for example. The adage "Garbage in, garbage out" is relevant when

collecting ratings, so it is critically important that the language used actually reflects the institutional structure, practices, and nomenclature. Consequently, the final version of each SAG presented to the reviewers is clearly labeled as being "edited for internal use at Longwood." As another internal decision, rather than encouraging the team members to come to consensus, all individual SAG ratings are averaged by the AVP. The self-study coordinator makes recommendations for the team, and final approval rests with the AVP. Team members are selected with intended diverse representation from students, faculty, staff, and in some cases, community members; some are chosen because of an intimate familiarity with the office and its functions; and others are more distantly associated. Unique and diverse perspectives are encouraged.

The assessment team also determines thresholds for evaluating the criterion and component averages, and those thresholds dictate what happens next. Given the four-point SAG rating of 0 to 3, an average rating of 2.0 or higher indicates an area of program strength, as the standards were deemed as having been "met" or "exceeded." Any rating averaging 1.9 or lower indicates that a standard was only "partially met" or "not met," which prompts an action plan for addressing that short-coming. Having staff input into the review process has increased buy-in and cooperation in what is often perceived by directors as a laborious, time-consuming process.

The following strategies have been helpful in providing clarity to the self-study process:

- Articulate the purpose of the review as well as the roles and responsibilities for all parties involved in the CAS self-study process (see Appendix A). Dispel any fears regarding any negative consequences based on results, and clarify the need for respecting differing individual perspectives as well as agreed-upon meeting times and deadlines.

- "Start with the end in mind" by providing all assessment team members with a copy of the *CAS Review Executive Summary and Action Plan* (see Appendix B). This allows reviewers to see how the individual ratings will be used and why their comments and responses to the overview questions are so critical to the process. It also helps to clarify deadlines and definitions, and provides some interpretation of the rating scale.

CHALLENGES ENCOUNTERED WITH IMPLEMENTATION

Student affairs practitioners are typically "doers" by nature: they juggle multiple roles and taxing workloads with little time and opportunity for reflection and planning. Students continually present with issues and concerns that require immediate attention. Consequently, systematizing a review process across professionally defined standards is essential for sustaining programs and services of quality, and ultimately, student learning and success.

Assessment team members often feel inadequately positioned to properly evaluate the details of a program's leadership, organizational structure, financial resources, etc. Furthermore, they often express trepidation or concern that a program's funding and/or the continued employment of personnel depend on the study's findings; consequently, comments and ratings should not be individually identifiable. Lastly, reviewers often fall into the trap of evaluating documentation rather than the actual program and service.

When funding is limited or flat, directors often battle the sentiment that nothing or little ever changes as a result of their review efforts. They also express fatigue and disappointment in reconciling ratings that repeatedly fall below expectations because of limited staffing and resources.

GENERAL RECOMMENDATIONS FROM
THE VPSA PERSPECTIVE

Designate a mid- to senior-level staff member within student affairs to provide leadership (and continuity) to the development and assessment of program service objectives and student learning outcomes, with oversight of the program review process. This senior-level staff member contributes an administrative influence and can prove instrumental in forming a diverse and willing assessment team for new directors who have not yet made connections with campus and community partners.

The creation of an assessment team—with representatives from all staffing groups across student affairs—to help oversee, support, and facilitate ongoing assessment will help to create a culture of evidence and a unit disposition driven by learning outcomes and continuous improvement. Soliciting the team's input into decisions regarding the CAS self-study process helps solidify support and clarify expectations for the process.

CHALLENGES AND RECOMMENDATIONS FOR
SMALL TO MEDIUM INSTITUTIONS

At Longwood and other small to medium colleges and universities, several departments and program areas have responsibility for multiple functions. Some are understaffed, while others rely heavily on assistance from paid and/or volunteer student staff. Consequently, when one office handles the functions outlined in two separate standards, the AVP can work with the self-study coordinator to edit the respective SAGs into one document to be utilized for the review process. For example, in lieu of two separate reviews of all 12 component area standards related to the Student Conduct Programs and Sexual Violence-Related Programs and Services areas, one consolidated review document was prepared using selected duplicated component areas, because both of these functions are performed by the same office and staff at Longwood. To further improve clarity for the reviewer and relevancy to Longwood's context, other edits to the in-house consolidated SAG were made that involved using the "search and replace" function to substitute the term "employee" with "volunteer student board member," since Longwood's conduct and disciplinary boards are run by student volunteers rather than staff or employees.

REPORTING PROCESS

With input from the student affairs assessment team, a template for the *CAS Review Executive Summary and Action Plan* was created (see Appendix B) to include the following elements: responses to the overview questions from each of the 12 component areas; areas of program strength, weakness, and ratings of "Does Not Apply" (DNA), "Insufficient Evidence" (IE), and those with significant discrepancies; descriptions of practices/issues requiring follow-up; specific actions, in priority order, required for the program to meet standards; and general recommendations for program enhancement. This report is ultimately reviewed by the department heads and VPSA, and feedback is shared accordingly.

In a staff meeting of all student affairs professionals, time is set aside for the previous year's self-study coordinators to present the most salient findings from their review. This provides both a relevant audience and a learning opportunity for those staff members unfamiliar with the CAS program review process. Additionally, past self-study coordinators are invited into a student affairs assessment team meeting with upcoming directors who are about to launch their own reviews, for a "lessons learned" discussion and orientation to the process.

Comparisons of departmental ratings are compiled in the aggregate and reviewed by the senior-level student affairs staff to determine overall trends and patterns of results. This 30,000-foot analysis of results has broader implications for strategic initiatives, budgeting, and professional development.

BENEFITS OF THE CAS STANDARDS FROM THE VPSA PERSPECTIVE

The single greatest benefit of using the CAS standards from an executive-level perspective is secured credibility, both internally and externally. Internally, department leadership gain perspective and clarity in discerning areas worthy of increased effort and resources. Choices as to what is "nice" and what is "necessary" are made clear, which can be helpful when determining priorities. Clarity on which services are essential is especially helpful for the VPSA when he or she is planning, budgeting, and allocating resources. The CAS approach helps to give all divisional leaders a broader perspective and often illuminates the need for intentional collaboration and shared staffing patterns. With the inherent turnover among staff, CAS self-studies provide student affairs leadership with the proper language and priorities needed to tweak evolving job descriptions in order to accurately reflect current and anticipated needs. Particularly at smaller and rural institutions, student affairs staff arrive with varying educational backgrounds and professional experience, so preparing for a CAS self-study serves as a primer and orientation to the field, especially when coupled with a study of the *Professional Competencies for Student Affairs Educators* (ACPA–College Student Educators International & NASPA–Student Affairs Administrators in Higher Education, 2015). This experience serves to bolster confidence and morale as well as to improve staff effectiveness.

As student affair practitioners, we rarely miss an opportunity to educate faculty, administration, and governing board members about the role student affairs plays in contributing to student learning and success. The primary purpose of CAS is to promote the improvement of programs and services that enhance the quality of student learning and development, which is clearly emphasized in the assessment team orientation. The VPSA seeks all possible chances to promote the division's use of the standards in the president's executive cabinet meetings and in reports to the board of trustees, which again raises perceptions of credibility from all campus constituents. And finally, student affairs organizations that use the CAS standards gain credibility from peer institutions, which is important in attracting qualified staff and in developing upward mobility of staff.

The past 5 years at Longwood have been witness to extensive changes, both in structure and in leadership, yet through the upheaval student affairs has remained the proverbial steady island in the stream. The use of the CAS materials has served as an anchor and has positioned the division well when it needs to respond to shifting internal and external currents and demands for accountability. Also noteworthy, Longwood successfully survived a recent reaffirmation of accreditation with no recommendations, which is in part attributed to the consistent application and review of externally defined professional expectations. A summary and action plan following program review periods—an often overlooked stage when managing institutional improvement—closes the loop and ensures that the CAS review is productive and remains a sound investment of energy and resources.

REFERENCE

ACPA–College Student Educators International & NASPA–Student Affairs Administrators in Higher Education. (2015). *Professional competency areas for student affairs educators.* Retrieved from http://www.naspa.org/images/uploads/main/ACPA_NASPA_Professional_Competencies_FINAL.pdf

Chapter 4

Using the CAS Standards for Divisionwide Program Review
The Case of a Regional Institution

Mary-Jeanne Raleigh and John R. Jones III

Regional universities serve a clear function in the U.S. higher education system. The mission of this type of institution is not just to educate but to serve the local community—and to advance quality of life through the execution of the university's mission. In the institution's vision statement, Dr. Robin Cummings, chancellor of the University of North Carolina–Pembroke (UNCP), summed up the mission of a regional university as "changing lives through education." Specifically, regional universities focus on serving the county and state in which they are located and, typically, they concentrate on undergraduate education and master's degrees. This simple definition encompasses many different types of university settings but perhaps relates most to that of UNCP. UNCP was the first college in the country designated for the education of Lumbee tribe members, and it prides itself on serving the Native Americans of southeastern North Carolina. This focus is an integral part of UNCP's identity and part of what makes this regional university incredibly unique.

The campus culture and the institution's mission are shaped by these Lumbee roots.

Guided by the accrediting standards of the Southern Association of Colleges and Schools (SACS) and the university's assessment plans, identifying goals and assessment processes fell under the division of student affairs for decades. However, in fall 2013, as a result of new leadership, the Council for the Advancement of Standards in Higher Education (CAS) materials were introduced by the vice chancellor of student affairs as a component of divisionwide strategic planning. The goal behind using the CAS model was to develop a divisionwide culture of assessment and, more specifically, to link internal and external department reviews to the creation of a strategic plan focused on learning outcomes. The movement from a SACS-based accreditation assessment plan to an internally motived process that reflects learning outcomes allowed the division to more clearly shape strategic planning. By developing a culture of evaluation and linking learning outcomes to the strategic plan, the division enhanced services and programs, promoted accountability, and advanced student success.

This chapter discusses the steps taken not only to introduce the CAS standards to the student affairs division but also, more important, to train the directors on using the standards to improve the quality of services and incorporate focused learning outcomes into each department's annual goals.

BEGINNING THE PROCESS

During the first year of implementation, the director of counseling and psychological services and the vice chancellor for student affairs started assessing the professional staff's level of apprehension toward departmental reviews. With those apprehensions in mind, training started with an introduction to the CAS philosophy and standards.

These training sessions, completed in less than 18 months, also laid the foundation of how to conduct an internal review. Trainings were cross-functional—that is, professional staff began to learn more about their colleagues' work and how departments contribute to the overall mission of the university.

Once all training sessions were completed, a pilot internal assessment was run with two departments' materials. Directors were divided into two groups. One group reviewed the material for Career Services; the other, Greek Life. In-house worksheets were designed to allow each department to collect information in formats that translated easily to the CAS review design. After all training workshops were completed and action plans developed for the completed department internal assessments, an informal survey on the lessons learned was conducted. The most important aspect of this process was the buy-in from directors and associate/assistant vice chancellors. They were asked to incorporate the CAS standards into the language of their work and, even more important, incorporate a focus on learning outcomes into their daily work lives.

ASSESSING READINESS

When a new procedure that sounds a lot like another layer of performance evaluation is introduced, some resistance is typical, even expected. Setting the tone and keeping a positive focus are critical for a review to overcome any initial trepidation. One of the many benefits of the CAS model is its focus on empowering the department through self-assessment. Ideally, this is the opportunity for the department—through the comparison to the CAS standards—to validate challenges, unearth unknown concerns, and spotlight strengths. In therapy, counselors and clients strive to develop insight, which allows clients to make changes, celebrate success, and strengthen needed skills to increase future resilience. This analogy demonstrates the philosophic core of the CAS standards: departments and overall divisions develop insight into their overall functioning, develop plans to make needed changes, and strengthen themselves.

Prochaska and DiClementi's change model (Conner, DiClementi, Valesquez, & Donovan, 2015) outlines the five stages people go through on their way to change, and this model can help to prepare the staff and the department/division for a successful CAS assessment. The majority of our directors moved easily from the precontemplation to the contemplation stage; the workshops helped to address the stages of preparation, action, and maintenance. Across any division or department you are likely to find individuals at varying stages of readiness to change. The model helps you not only to determine which stage a person is in but also to motivate the person to sustain that change. Before 2013, only a handful of the student affairs professionals at UNCP had exposure to the CAS standards, and still fewer had used the material in any assessment function. In truth, none of the professional staff were considering using the CAS model for a formal review of services. After conversations with department leaders, it became clear that directors were afraid that the CAS assessment really meant a performance evaluation or—worse—would translate into lost jobs and/or lost wages. The majority of the team was in the precontemplation stage; few were in early contemplation.

To prepare the division for the execution of a full-scale CAS assessment, we first needed to alleviate the concerns. The very first workshop for the division was on the CAS philosophy, and throughout this workshop we reinforced the focus on supporting and collaborating with colleagues. We did so partly to address the fears expressed and to also increase a sense of cohesion within the group. In fact, this positive disposition was reinforced in all our CAS sessions. Once the CAS preparation sessions were done, the feeling of the group toward the

CAS process shifted. "Through CAS training and preparing for the assessment, the appreciation and understanding of the scope of the learning outcomes as well as the complexity of the services we provide are increasing in the division," reflected Robert Candida (personal communication, May 15, 2016), director of the Office of Diversity and Inclusion at UNCP.

LAYING THE FOUNDATION

A series of five 60- and 90-minute workshops were conducted with all student affairs directors. The series included such topics as introduction to the CAS standards, benchmarking, writing strategic goals, writing learning outcomes, and methods of data collection. This series began in January 2014 with a workshop on the CAS standards and benchmarking. The goal of these workshops was to prepare the student affairs directors for a pilot training process in the upcoming semester. The vice chancellor of student affairs chose two departments to undergo the pilot CAS internal review. Directors and assistant directors from each of the student affairs departments were required to attend all training sessions as preparation for the strategic initiative that included a CAS review.

A student affairs strategic planning initiative that started in the fall and extended over the academic year included the development of a goal worksheet to assist in the creation of department and expanded division goals. Because the worksheet had green headings and green blocks to fill in the layout, the form was affectionately referred to as "green sheets" (see Appendix C). From their creation, the green sheets included a section on learning outcomes. This section was not required to be completed in the first year but was included to help staff become comfortable with the language and the concept of learning outcomes. Having the learning outcomes on the sheet set the expectation of identifying clear, measurable goals and evaluating student learning. Learning outcomes became a required part of every strategic initiative the following academic year, the second year of the division CAS assessment cycle.

During a summer retreat, a series of workshops covered the key elements of executing an internal assessment. After understanding the readiness of the division and department leaders, workshops were designed with these specific topics: benchmarking, type of benchmarking, writing goals, defining student learning outcomes, and collecting qualitative and quantitative measures of learning and data. Each student affairs division in any college or university will need to assess not only readiness but also gaps in education before a meaningful CAS review can be launched. A tacit goal that we had hoped to accomplish was to generate enthusiasm and a positive attitude toward the CAS process and what it can bring to each department and the division as a whole. A secondary goal from the CAS review was pointed out by Cora Bullard (personal communication, May 18, 2016), UNCP's director of Student Health Services (SHS): "I have found the CAS review, internal and external, to be very helpful in getting procedures changed for SHS. One example is the hours of operations for our office. Once we received the internal CAS review and completed benchmarking, we were able to align our hours with other SHS centers."

Depending on the division and the level of knowledge about assessment from department leaders, the type of training will need to be determined, and it will likely be multilayered. Benchmarking, understanding CAS rubrics, setting measurable goals, designing department objectives, incorporating institutional vision and mission into CAS action plans, setting external reviews and experts, assimilating learning outcomes language into the division culture, and, finally, aligning learning outcomes goals with the department/division and institutional missions are essential to the development of a meaningful assessment protocol. The time and attention given to each aspect of assessment will be determined by the institution's leadership. There is no lockstep sequence for how and when to train staff in each of these topics; however, it is important that each element is understood.

PILOTING A TRAINING REVIEW

One of the first steps in creating a culture of assessment is to train as many members of the student affairs leadership team as possible in the steps of a CAS internal review. Small assessment teams are desirable, but in order to train many staff quickly, larger teams must be used. To train individuals in how to conduct an internal review, a step-by-step breakdown should be conducted over three meetings. In our case, the first meeting included a review of how to read the CAS standards and guidelines, and we practiced using the rating scales. This was critical, in order to increase inter-rater reliability and accuracy of the feedback given to the department under review. Although Career Services and Greek Life were the two departments selected to participate in the CAS internal review training, the results from the training were still useful and meaningful for the entire division.

Material submitted by the departments to support the review was introduced during the first training meeting. The second meeting was conducted 3 weeks later and focused on ranking each area of the standard with the material submitted. The primary focus of the second meeting was to discuss any discrepancies in individuals' rankings of the material. This was an important step in reinforcing the positive perspective of the CAS internal review. We also practiced framing feedback in action-oriented steps that would clearly lead to positive change. Our third and final meeting focused on reviewing the internal review report and generating suggestions for an action plan. The departments being reviewed for the training were offered the option to meet with the review team and discuss the report. If the department wanted a summary meeting, the time was spent generating both an action plan and suggestions for the external review timeline.

The pilot training concluded with soliciting feedback on the process from both teams. The two departments under review were encouraged to only use the material from the training as a guide and to have a proper, in-depth internal review in the near future. Feedback from participants indicated that the size of the training groups (15+ members) were too large and hampered a deeper understanding of the CAS process. From our experience, it is recommended that you identify a smaller internal review team, chaired by a student affairs director from a different department. For the student affairs division at UNCP, each team has representation from students, faculty, the department under review, and a graduate student.

CROSS-FUNCTIONAL TRAINING

No less than once a semester, a CAS review session is held for departments prior to their internal review and for the directors chairing the review itself. Each department is locked into a 5-year assessment cycle: year 1, establish benchmarks and prepare the material needed for a CAS review; year 2, conduct a CAS internal review and develop an action plan; year 3, conduct an external review and adjust the action plan, if needed; year 4, enact the action plan and continue data collection; year 5, prep for an internal review. The assessment cycle is set up to allow a director to chair another department's review a semester prior to his or her own department review. This allows the chair to prepare his or her own department for its review. Feedback from staff about this process has been very positive. The department heading into review is assured the chair is well trained and understands the work necessary to prepare material for the internal review.

Allowing colleagues to support and conduct department reviews within the division has proven to be a great way not only to enhance change and increase awareness of other departments but also to build cohesion. After completing the review of Student Health Services, the chair of the review team better understood the work of Student Health Services and was able to advocate for that department. The Counseling and Psychological Services (CAPS) associate director served as the chair for the Student Health Services internal review. During a recent meeting with police and public safety, the CAPS associate director was able to articulate the importance of having additional nursing staff, advocate for a colleague in that department, and understand the challenges and strengths of the clinical health staff. A staff member from Orientation and Student Leadership chaired the internal review of the Office of Diversity and Inclusion. She later commented about developing a new understanding of the multiple collaborative links the two departments shared. This increasing insight into the work and needs of other departments has resulted in a more connected and collaborative division of student affairs.

An additional benefit to this type of cross-functional training is that each director has a more clear understanding of the professional standards in multiple offices. This structure also allowed each director to practice creating goal-focused measureable action plans. The professional development of all student affairs members is an added bonus; all student affairs professional staff can talk knowledgably about how to conduct an internal review.

ORGANIC DEVELOPMENT OF FORMS AND ELEMENTS

At the end of the second year of the divisionwide assessment process, it became clear that an assessment oversight and training committee was needed. Subsequently, a student affairs assessment committee was formed in fall 2015. The charge of this committee includes the ongoing training of review chairs, preparation of departments for review, support in the execution of an external review, data collection guidance, and design of forms and templates for the process. The chair of the assessment committee, working with committee members, conducts training, creates appropriate documents, and incorporates feedback in all aspects of the CAS review process.

The original green sheets were modified after feedback from the entire division. One change involved adding a reference section to the second page of the worksheet. The references include the university vision and mission, the values outlined by the university chancellor, and the CAS student learning outcomes. The division vision, mission, goals, and objectives are also included in the reference material, with every objective designed by the departments themselves. Each department is encouraged to create no fewer than two learning-directed objectives. Also, each department needs to create at least three annual procedure or resource development objectives. Monthly reports require an update from each department on goals, objectives, and learning outcomes. These reports also ask for information on collaborative efforts, professional advancements, future programming, and outreach efforts. Monthly reports were specifically redesigned to include CAS learning outcomes and to feed directly into the annual year-end report (see Appendix D) and year-end summary (see Appendix E).

CLOSING THE LOOP

Educational sessions are made available throughout the academic year and as needed at the request of specific departments. Commitment of the administration is imperative: more than just purchasing the CAS materials, the administration needs to commit people, time, and resources to the cycle of assessment. Training of new staff is critical in keeping an understanding of CAS assessment as a part of the campus culture.

In the last year of the CAS review cycle, the entire division will be involved in an external review. The external reviewers will need to have appropriate professional competencies, represent sister institutions, and have multiple administrative levels. The purpose of this last step is to explore how the division as a whole meets and/or exceeds the standards across all of the departments within the division and to address any shortcomings missed by the internal review.

CONCLUSION

Any division looking at creating a 5-year review cycle using the CAS model should anticipate resistance and embrace enthusiasm. Make the final report of the internal review available to all stakeholders, and allow the external reviewers access to the action plan designed by the department from the internal review. Underscore and support the positive uses of the information, and tackle any negative use of the CAS assessment process with advocacy for the department. Student affairs departments starting a CAS review should keep in mind this valuable advice from UNCP's Director of the Office of Student Involvement and Leadership Michael Severy (personal communication, May 24, 2016): "While it's affirming to go line by line and acknowledge the successes, that [step] was quickly bypassed to focus on the areas for improvement. Be sure to create the time and space in the process to dwell on what you and your staff did well and cultivate the possibility that exists in those areas, too."

REFERENCE

Conner, G. J., DiClementi, C. C., Valesquez, M. M., & Donovan, D. M. (2015). *Substance abuse treatment and the stages of change*. New York, NY: Guilford Press.

Chapter 5

Using the CAS Standards
With a Whole Division
A Student Affairs Assessment Officer's View

Jennifer Wells

As other chapters in this book demonstrate, there are many ways to implement the Council for the Advancement of Standards in Higher Education (CAS) materials at colleges and universities, including self-study, program reviews, and measures of effectiveness. This chapter is written from my perspective as a student affairs assessment officer working at the division level. This chapter outlines the history of infusing the CAS standards into the culture of a division and will highlight creative approaches to implementation.

INSTITUTIONAL CONTEXT

Kennesaw State University (KSU) began as a junior college in 1963 with a first-year enrollment of about 1,000 students. In 1976, KSU became a 4-year college and graduated its first 4-year class in 1980. By 1990, there were more than 10,000 students; in 1996, KSU achieved its university status. On January 6, 2015, the Board of Regents of the University System of Georgia approved the consolidation of Kennesaw

State University and Southern Polytechnic State University. The goal was to create a single, integrated institution that has two main campuses. KSU is now a doctoral research institution with R3 (Moderate Research Activity) and Community Engagement Carnegie Classifications. With approximately 33,000 students, it is the third-largest university in Georgia and offers more than 150 undergraduate and doctoral and graduate degrees. The rapid growth of KSU is important in providing institutional context and perspective for student affairs at KSU.

I started at KSU as the director of assessment for the Division of Student Success (now Student Affairs) in May 2011. The vice president for student affairs created the position in response to the increased pressure for accountability and need to provide evidence of effectiveness. I was charged with writing new mission and vision statements, learning outcomes, and a strategic plan for the division. Inherent in this charge was the hope that a culture of assessment could be infused in the division. Prior to my arrival, the CAS standards were not being broadly used. During my interview, I discussed infusing the CAS approach into the division, as it would provide the opportunity for a "universal language," a common approach to assessment, and additional assessment resources. I formed a committee with cross-representation from the division and undertook these tasks. After drafting new vision and mission statements, the committee focused on developing learning outcomes. We researched other divisions of student affairs' learning outcomes, focusing on those at peer and aspirational institutions. As described in *CAS Professional Standards for Higher Education* (CAS, 2015), we found that there were many similar themes and values across institutions, resources, and CAS as an organization. With this information, and after reviewing the CAS learning and development outcomes, we decided to adopt them in full as the division's learning outcomes.

With a new mission, vision, and set of learning outcomes, the committee began drafting a strategic plan. During the first 2 months, I met with individuals from every unit in the division to build relationships and understand the breadth of their work. During these meetings we discussed areas they wanted to assess and improve. I shared the themes from these conversations with the committee. In addition, the committee reviewed several example strategic plans from other student affairs divisions. Four strategic goals emerged from our research and discussions and were used to focus the strategic plan. The strategic plan incorporated the CAS approach in two main ways. The first was in reference to ensuring that students were achieving the learning outcomes; the second was in support of improving operational efficiency and effectiveness. Because of its reputation for quality standards written with a consensus approach and supported by guiding principles, the CAS standards were identified as one of the vehicles by which units could conduct comprehensive audits. Those who had experience and knowledge with the CAS standards easily bought in to their inclusion. Others eventually did so as well; I think this was either because once they learned more, they recognized the value inherent in the CAS approach or because of the relationships and trust I had built in those early weeks. In the end, the CAS standards were included in the strategic plan as shown in Figure 5.1 (bold added).

Figure 5.1. **Examples of Standards Used and Adjusted**

Goal 1: Create and strengthen partnerships with students to provide diverse, holistic learning experiences beyond the classroom.

Outcome 3: **Ensure that students are achieving the CAS *Learning and Development* outcomes relevant to their individual success.**

Goal 4: Expand resources and improve operational efficiency and effectiveness for the Division for Student Success.

Outcome 2: Optimize business processes, organizational structure, and program effectiveness.

Action Step 1: **Conduct comprehensive audits for two to three departments/ units per year using two or more of the following: CAS standards,** USG Standards, and national/state functional area standards; conduct KSU internal audit.

In fall 2013, the president's cabinet approved the division's strategic plan. Approximately a week later, it was announced that KSU and Southern Polytechnic State University would consolidate. While this was a very exciting decision, it did cause the newly approved division strategic plan to be placed on hold.

CONSOLIDATION

Consolidation provided the opportunity to recreate programs and services in the division. Across the new institution, the consolidation process included more than 700 specific responsibilities that were assigned to 81 operational working groups (OWGs) and 22 areas. Each area was represented by an area coordinator who was a member of the consolidation implementation committee (CIC), which oversaw the entire process and decision making around consolidation. To scaffold the work of such a large merger, the OWGs created recommendations that were submitted and ultimately approved by the CIC. The Division of Student Affairs at KSU was represented in 14 OWGs: Advising, Mentoring, and Tutoring; International Programs; Diversity and Inclusion Programs and Activities; Competition Teams (Non-Sports); Club Sports, Intramurals, and Recreational Sports; Greek Life; Preserving Traditions and History; Registered Student Organizations; Student Government Association; Career Services; Counseling; Disability Services and Testing; Housing; and Student Conduct and Academic Integrity.

For each of the areas listed above, I provided the group with the functional area CAS standards to assist in the consolidation process. The OWGs were not required to use the standards, but they were encouraged to use the relevant standards in their planning meetings. Each set of CAS standards is comprised of 12 subsections (see Chapter 1). The OWGs were encouraged to use these subsections as topics for discussion and direction. For example, what is the mission of our area? What programs should be offered? How should we be structured? How do you integrate programs from two campuses? What are the major considerations? What should the program or service be called?

THINKING OUTSIDE THE CAS STANDARDS BOX

During my time as the director of planning and assessment (my original position with the institution), I tried to infuse the CAS approach into the work of the division because of my prior experience working with CAS. At that time, CAS had a 30-year history of a consensus-based approach to standards development and representation of nearly 40 member associations. I knew the CAS standards could be used for self-study and self-regulation, design of new programs and services, professional development, academic and professional preparation, credibility and accountability, and institutional-level program review (CAS, 2015). This section provides examples of how KSU "thought outside the CAS box" in its use of the learning and development outcomes, functional area standards, and self-assessment guides.

Learning and Development Outcomes

CAS demonstrates support for student learning by including learning outcomes in the General Standards, and therefore they appear in all functional area standards. The student learning and development model includes six broad categories, called domains: knowledge acquisition, construction, integration and application; cognitive complexity; intrapersonal development; interpersonal development; humanitarianism and civic engagement; and practical competence. Each domain contains dimensions, which further clarify the outcome areas. During my tenure, the domains and dimensions were incorporated in many different ways and helped guide the work of many programs and services.

Each summer, all units in the Division of Student Affairs are required to submit an annual report, which includes information about the unit, descriptions of each unit's current assessment initiatives, program objectives and learning outcomes, points of pride/major accomplishments, and how the unit/department supports the university's strategic plan. Furthermore, units are asked to list programs, services, and initiatives, and to align them with the CAS domains and dimensions addressed (see Figure 5.2).

Figure 5.2 **Annual Report Template for Unit Learning and Development Outcomes**

Learning Outcomes →	Knowledge Acquisition, Construction, Integration, and Application				Cognitive Complexity				Intrapersonal Development				Interpersonal Development				Humanitarianism and Civic Engagement				Practical Competence							
Program/Initiative →	1	2	3	4	5	6	7	8	9	10	11	12	13	14	15	16	17	18	19	20	21	22	23	24	25	26	27	28

As units infused learning outcomes into their programs, I would walk them through an exercise using the CAS learning and development domains. I asked them to read through the examples of learning development outcomes (included in the CAS outcomes document) and to highlight all of the statements that most closely aligned with their intended objectives (see Figure 5.3). From there, we would talk about whether those example outcomes were directly or indirectly related. For example, in a program about developing leadership skills, a direct outcome might be "identifies and understands the dynamics of a group," and an indirect outcome might be "seeks involvement with people different from oneself." From there, we would adjust the language in the examples for internal usage and create an assessment of learning for the program, service, or initiative.

One particularly interesting example was in the Department of Student Life. Department members were in the process of restructuring their fall student organization leader training conference to incorporate more measurable learning and development experiences. The conference evaluation was built using the technique above. In the survey, conference participants were asked, using a Likert-type scale, to indicate their level of agreement with several statements—for example, "I seek the involvement of others." The results of the instrument helped the staff to improve the training by instituting a full-day conference with several breakout sessions, all focused on improving the students' leadership skills.

Figure 5.3. **Example of Objectives Within a Unit**

Collaboration	Works cooperatively with others, including people different from self and/or with different points of view; seeks and values the involvement of others; listens to and considers others' points of view
Effective leadership	Demonstrates skill in guiding and assisting a group, organization, or community in meeting its goals; identifies and understands the dynamics of a group; exhibits democratic principles as a leader or group member; communicates a vision, mission, or purpose that encourages commitment and action in others
Understanding and appreciation of cultural and human differences	Understands one's own identity and culture; seeks involvement with people different from oneself; articulates the advantages and impact of a diverse society; identifies systematic barriers to equality and inclusiveness, then advocates and justifies means for dismantling them; in interactions with others; exhibits respect and preserves the dignity of others

In the Center for Student Leadership, one staff member wanted to formalize the work of the peer leaders for first-year seminars. She was looking for a model that the peer leaders could use to help students in the classroom build a student leadership plan that would focus on out-of-class activities. She used the CAS learning and development outcomes as the foundation to build a program of study to help first-year students make plans and goals. She chose dimensions that aligned with intended outcomes in the first year and then designed activities/actions that students could do to make progress in that dimension. Using the practical competence domain as an example, the following shows how an action is matched with a specific learning dimension from that domain.

- Meet with a KSU personal trainer (Dimension: maintain health and wellness)
- Meet with career services for a résumé review (Dimension: managing career development)
- Keep and follow a detailed schedule (Dimension: managing personal affairs)

Additional dimensions—chosen from other domains but still relevant for the context—included identity development, meaningful relationships, and relating knowledge to daily life. Consistent with the idea of alignment through development, assessment, and adjustment continuum, there were many activities/actions listed for each dimension in the student leadership plan.

Under the leadership of the vice president for student affairs, the division adopted one of the domains, practical competence, as a universal learning outcome for the division. This was the first time in the history of the division that one universal learning focus was adopted across departments and units. After discussion of all six domains, the leadership team felt that, while all of them were important and applicable, the practical competence dimensions (pursuing goals, communicating effectively, technological competence, managing personal affairs, managing career development, demonstrating professionalism, maintaining health and wellness, living a purposeful and satisfying life) were the most universal across the diversity of units and missions in the division. Subsequently, every unit needed to identify and assess one outcome using a dimension in the practical competence domain. For example, a Career Services outcome is "increase student preparedness for the career fair," and one measure of this is the employer evaluation survey, given at the career fairs, asking specifically about their impressions of student preparedness.

Functional Area Standards

In my experience, there are many different ways to apply the functional areas standards; the first example of this was highlighted in the consolidation discussion earlier in the chapter. The functional area standards were given to the OWGs to help guide their discussions, assist in making recommendations, and provide direction for the new programs and services. While consolidation was the impetus for the review of the functional areas standards at KSU, the same approach can be used for other reasons, such as engaging in strategic planning processes, transitioning into a new position or department, creating a new unit or office, or training staff.

As a very specific example, the standards and guidelines can also be used to help decide the name of a unit. For example, the Women's Resource and Interpersonal Violence Prevention Center (WRIVPC) wanted to research and assess the appropriateness of the unit name. The CAS standards in this area are Women's and Gender Programs and Services, and Sexual Violence–Related Programs and Services. The purposes of these two areas are similar in that they both seek to create supportive and safe environments, as outlined in the standards for each. However, as the two statements from the functional areas standards below demonstrate, there are also differences in the missions of these two areas.

- "The purpose of Women's and Gender Programs and Services is to advance gender equity, educate the campus community about women's and gender issues, and promote a supportive and safe environment for women and all campus constituents facing gender-based oppression" (CAS, 2015, p. 493).
- "The mission of Sexual Violence–Related Programs and Services is to end sexual violence on campus and to engage the campus community in creating a safe, supportive, and responsive environment for all members affected when sexual violence occurs" (CAS, 2015, p. 410).

The interest in assessing the unit's name led to a review of the two relevant functional area standards, which then highlighted the importance of answering questions related to the mission of the unit, the needs of the students, how students use the services, and how students perceive the WRIVPC. Student focus groups were used as one component of answering this question and clarifying the priorities of the center.

Self-Assessment Guides

Self-Assessment Guides (SAGs) are provided for each set of standards and guidelines, and offer a "recommended, comprehensive self-study process for program evaluation" (CAS, 2015, p. 13). At KSU, the self-assessment process was implemented in a number of ways. There is a KSU Alcohol and Other Drugs Education and Prevention Coalition, which has a subgroup focused on programming and education on campus. The subgroup used the Alcohol and Other Drug Programs (AODP) SAG to help evaluate the effectiveness of the team's work. Of the 12 subsections of the standards, the subgroup chose to focus only on the program section, because it addresses what the functional area actually does; what resources, services, and activities are vital; and what functions serve as the cornerstone of the area. The standards in the program section aligned very closely with the charge and purpose of the work of the programming and education subgroup. Each member of the committee considered the criterion measures in the program section of the SAG and rated the degree to which the work of the subgroup was in alignment with the standards. For example, one of the standards states, "In development of programs and services, AODP must take into account evidence-based strategies; assessment, counseling, and referral; community collaboration; environmental management strategies; institutional policies; student leadership and involvement; stakeholder training and education; and biennial or other review as required by law" (CAS, 2015, p. 58). The ratings indicated that there was room for improvement in how the coalition implemented the suggested evidence-based strategies. At their next meeting, the coalition discussed the ratings and used the results to plan their programming and to address areas of improvement.

The interim director of Fraternity and Sorority Life (FSL) contacted me to help guide the office through a program review. I encouraged the interim director to be intentional about representation on the review committee—that is, to include individuals with a strong understanding of fraternities and sororities as well as individuals with only a limited or cursory knowledge. This range of perspectives helped to ensure the most comprehensive and objective review of the unit. As a result, the review committee included representatives from career services, orientation, the College of Education, the College of Humanities and Social Sciences, and the College of Business. I provided an overview and training for the CAS program review process, as outlined below.

- Overview of the CAS standards
- Applications for the CAS standards
- Twelve parts of the General Standards/all functional area standards
- Conducting self-assessment using the CAS standards
  - Fundamental elements about self-assessment
  - CAS evaluation steps (plan the process; assemble and educate team; identify, collect, and review evidence; conduct and interpret SAG ratings using evaluative evidence; develop an action plan; and prepare a report)
  - Review of the SAG
- Next steps
- Resources

FSL staff members collected the evidence and placed it in a shared electronic folder. Each individual committee member reviewed the evidence and completed the SAG ratings. As a review committee, they discussed discrepancies in ratings as well as the strengths and areas of improvement for FSL. This program review process served as a pilot for divisionwide implementation.

CONCLUSION

I have a saying that "CAS is your friend." The CAS standards provide directions and resources for usage, but the standards are not prescriptive—it is OK to be creative in how they are implemented. While the standards are meant to be universal and applicable across institutional types and sizes, there is no rigid one-size-fits-all approach. As described above, KSU has found multiple ways to infuse the CAS standards in student affairs; the examples represent just a portion or snapshot of the many ways in which the standards are used in the division and at our institution. CAS provides helpful resources that create a strong foundation for building a culture of assessment, data-driven decision making, and continuous improvement.

REFERENCE

Council for the Advancement of Standards in Higher Education. (2015). *CAS professional standards for higher education* (9th ed.). Washington, DC: Author.

Chapter 6

Using the CAS Standards in Academic Advising
The Community College Setting

Adrian Rodriguez and Louann Schulze

With more than 10 million students enrolled in U.S. community colleges, these institutions represent an important sector of higher education. Community college students make up 42% of all undergraduates nationwide (National Center for Education Statistics, 2015). Two thirds of community college students attend part time, and 51% of all students attending community colleges identify as an ethnicity other than White (American Association of Community Colleges, 2016). Many such colleges are large and complex, with multiple campuses offering student support and services. Thus, it is important to find ways to assess these various programs and services.

This chapter discusses how the Council for the Advancement of Standards in Higher Education (CAS) standards and approach were used to review the area of academic advising at a public multicampus community college district. The process is described through the lens of one campus's student development services leadership team, which participated in a comprehensive review of the Student Development Services Division for the entire district.

INSTITUTIONAL BACKGROUND

The Tarrant County College District (TCCD) is a comprehensive 2-year institution that was established as Tarrant County Junior College on July 31, 1965, in the Fort Worth area of north Texas. For more than 50 years, TCCD has provided quality education to the people of Tarrant County.

More than 50,000 students are in TCCD's associate degree and technical programs, making TCCD the sixth-largest institution among Texas colleges and universities. Community and industry education offers additional opportunities for businesses and individuals of all ages, through continuing education courses, workshops, and customized training programs.

Tarrant County College District is made up of six major campuses, including TCC Connect, a virtual campus accredited by the Southern Association of Colleges and Schools Commission on Colleges (SACSCOC) in 2015. TCCD is governed by a seven-member board of trustees.

With student success as a focal point of TCCD's Vision 2015 Strategic Plan, the district set forth initiatives and partnered with organizations to ensure student success. TCCD joined Achieving the Dream: Community Colleges Count and became an Achieving the Dream Leader College in 2014. TCCD also joined Project SSStrong (Supporting Student Success Transformations Reaching ONward to Graduation), a grant-funded program of the United States Department of Education.

INITIAL CONSIDERATIONS FOR THE CAS PROGRAM REVIEW PROCESS

While program reviews are common at community colleges for academic programs—particularly career, technical, and continuing education programs—comprehensive program reviews in the area of student support services are less prevalent. TCCD did not have a systemic approach for assessment and evaluation for the Student Development Services Division throughout its campuses.

In preparation for TCCD's reaffirmation of accreditation through the SACSCOC, it was necessary for student support services to create and implement a process for assessing its own student programs and services. A more formalized and systemic program review process would support TCCD's compliance with SACSCOC Core Requirement 2.10, which states, "The institution provides student support programs, services, and activities consistent with its mission that promote student learning and enhance the development of its students" (SACSCOC, 2009, p. 18). It would also need to comply with Comprehensive Standard 3.3.1.3, which focuses on institutional effectiveness in educational support services (SACSCOC, 2009).

To ensure the continuation of high-quality programs and support services, TCCD decided to use the standards established by CAS (2015) as a format for conducting program reviews. Because the CAS standards and approach are supported by more than 40 organizations, they are considered the leading and best practice in the field of program review for student support services. Using the CAS standards would also address Goal 3 of TCCD's Vision 2015 Strategic Plan, which focused on promoting institutional effectiveness, collaborating with the community, and creating an environment where employees are engaged in development.

This program review process was also seen as an opportunity to showcase exceptional programs and services offered on each campus that could potentially be scaled up districtwide, and to identify areas where improvements were needed, both on specific campuses and at the district level. Since the Vision 2015 Strategic Plan and the SACSCOC accreditation were managed by district personnel, the charge for student support services program review was also championed by the district via the Office of the Vice Chancellor for Student Success. Though spearheaded by the district, the program review depended on the respective campus leaders of each functional area to work together to carry it out. Therefore, the district provided thorough training and guidelines for executing the CAS program review process to the campuses.

CAS AT TARRANT COUNTY COLLEGE DISTRICT

The student development services departments received direction from the vice chancellor for student success communicating the intent and plan for the program review. The offices within the Divisions of Student Development Services and Student Success to be reviewed were academic advising, disability support services, information center, student support services (TRiO), student conduct programs, career and employment services, counseling, campus activities, registrar, testing, health services, upward bound, and financial aid. Due to the many areas to be reviewed—and the need to employ many of the same personnel for multiple reviews—it was determined that the review process would be conducted in two separate cycles: fall and spring. This would also ensure that TCCD had 2 years of process data prior to the submission deadlines for reaffirmation of accreditation. Recognizing that some program reviews would be more involved than others, the offices/areas of student support were divided across both cycles and engaged in the program review process. The teams utilized a continuous improvement model that included program evaluation using the CAS standards. The model also directed implementation of an action plan for the evaluation—inclusive of collection and review of data—and continuous quality improvement.

Included in the instruction to the student development services departments were the identified program review chair(s) for each functional area: the campus vice presidents for student development services as well as other district directors. These program review chairs were to work directly with the functional area chairs, who were not yet identified, to conduct the program review for each functional area identified. The functional area chair's responsibilities were to lead in the identification of component areas to be reviewed; to lead in the identification, coordination, and communication to two evaluators for the respective functional area; to lead in the collection of the evidence/ data for the program review; and to lead in the execution of the CAS program review process and the development and implementation of the action plan for the functional area.

In preparation for the initial training, the program review chair worked with the respective campus leaders for each functional area to identify those components that would be a part of the program review process. The complete list of component areas considered as part of the TCCD assessment process is: mission; program; leadership; human resources; ethics; legal responsibility; equity and access; diversity; organization and management; campus and external relations; financial resources; technology; facilities and equipment; and assessment and evaluation. All student development areas had six common component areas—mission, program, leadership, organization and management, campus and external relations, and assessment and evaluation—seen as fundamental to the assessment process and as a means to provide consistency for all functional areas. In addition to those six components, each functional area identified two more components likely to provide the most benefit to the functional area.

Each functional area also identified at least one student learning outcome to focus on as part of the program review process. The functional area described how the selected student learning outcome was achieved and provided evidence that demonstrated such achievement. The student learning outcomes (domains and dimensions) as specified in the CAS standards are listed in Appendix F. As an example, the directors of academic advising determined that the knowledge acquisition, integration, construction, and application domain as well as the practical competence domain were extremely relevant to the goals of academic advising at TCCD. Thus, the directors focused on these domains and dimensions as they developed an action plan for their areas.

Each functional area selected a separate program review evaluation team comprised of faculty, staff, and administrators who were not associated with the area under review; we did this to prevent bias based on familiarity with the functional area. Each evaluation team was required to include at least one administrator and one faculty member, and the administrator was required to be at the coordinator/director level or higher. Our procedure and recommendation is that each evaluation team be no less than three people and no more than five. Those from external organizations could be included as part of the program review evaluation team, provided they completed the required training.

Two initial half-day program review trainings were conducted for the departmental personnel, program review chairs, and functional area chairs. Subsequent trainings were provided for evaluators. The initial training focused on the need for self-assessment and program review, the expected results of the program review process, the way to use the CAS standards and approach a review of the Self-Assessment Guides (SAGs), the way to prepare for the evaluation sessions and the types of evidence to collect, the way to create reports and an action plan, and methods to engage others in the program improvement process.

A follow-up session was conducted specifically for the areas to be reviewed as part of Cycle 1 (fall) but was also open to those who would be participating in Cycle 2 (spring). A program review evaluator training was also held; it was designed specifically for those participating in the program review process as an evaluation team member. The areas/offices of student support assessed and their component areas are shown in Table 6.1.

Table 6.1. **Student Support Areas/Offices Assessed and Component Areas**

Cycle 1		
Area	**District Component Areas**	**Additional Component Areas**
Academic Advising	Mission	Human Resources and Diversity
	Program	
Disability Support Services	Leadership	Human Resources and Diversity
Information Center	Organization and Management	Technology and Diversity
Student Support Services (TRiO)	Campus and External Relations	Diversity and Financial Resources
Student Conduct Programs	Assessment and Evaluation	Ethics and Legal Responsibilities
Career and Employment Services		Technology and Facilities and Equipment
Cycle 2		
Counseling	Mission	Human Resources and Diversity
	Program	
Student Development Services (Student Activities)	Leadership	Legal Responsibility and Diversity
Registrar	Organization and Management	Equity and Access and Diversity
Testing	Campus and External Relations	Ethics and Equity and Access
Health Services	Assessment and Evaluation	Legal Responsibilities and Technology
Upward Bound		Equity and Access and Financial Resources
Financial Aid		Technology and Equity and Access

USING THE CAS STANDARDS IN ACADEMIC ADVISING

At TCCD, as is the case at many community colleges, the functions of academic advising and counseling are in the same office. There is often overlap with the counselors, who are called upon not only to provide counseling services but also to give academic advising when the need demands.

At the beginning of the program review process, the directors of academic advising recommended to the vice presidents for student development services that academic advising and counseling be separated for the purposes of the program review process. Since these functions are listed separately and have a separate set of standards, this was an easy decision. Academic advising would be assessed in the first cycle (fall) and counseling services would be assessed in the second (spring). At TCCD, each campus has a director of counseling who provides oversight to academic advisement, career services, counseling, disability support services, testing, and the transfer center. There is some variance in the areas of supervision, as a few directors also oversee a Veterans Center and a New Student Welcome Center. While the official title for the position is the "director of counseling," we use the title "director of academic advising" throughout this chapter to simplify its relationship to academic advising. These five directors of academic advising make up the functional area team for academic advising programs, because the program review is being done for TCCD's academic advising programs as a whole.

The 2009 CAS SAG for academic advising programs included 14 component areas. Given the abbreviated timeline for completing the process, the district selected 6 component areas to be assessed and gave the unit directors the opportunity to select 2 additional component areas. As previously stated, the district charged every unit with assessing mission, program, leadership, organization and management, campus and external relations, and assessment and evaluation. The directors of academic advising selected diversity and human resources as the additional areas to be assessed; the main reason for selecting the diversity component area was to perform a gap analysis and to identify any potential areas of concern. This inclusion also allowed for the directors of academic advising to examine their staff demographics and to evaluate TCCD's current initiatives in providing academic advising services to students of color. The team identified the human resources component area in an effort to evaluate the effectiveness of the current staffing of full-time and part-time personnel in academic advising across the district. The directors of academic advising felt that diversity and human resources were the most critical component areas relative to serving the student population.

Regarding the student learning outcomes (domains and dimensions), the directors of academic advising focused on the knowledge acquisition, integration, construction, and application domain as well as the practical competence domain. The directors identified a set of practical goals with intended outcomes aligned to these domains and dimensions. These included declaring a major; establishing an educational plan; meeting the requirements of the Texas Success Initiative Assessment areas of reading, writing, and math; being in good academic standing; and completing 30 semester hours. When students complete the identified learning outcomes, they are no longer required to meet with an academic advisor. As a result of this work, Tarrant County College began requiring all first-time-in-college (FTIC) students to visit with an academic advisor two times during their first year of college. Since then, TCCD data has shown that students visiting with an academic advisor two or more times were retained at a higher rate than students who visited with an advisor less than two times throughout their first year. Although this level of commitment for high enrollment institutions can put a strain on resources in the academic advising area, this intervention can also positively affect persistence, retention, and student success for first-year students.

The academic advising functional team consisted of the five campus directors of academic advising. The team met at the Trinity River campus, TCCD's new downtown, most central, site. In an effort to meet the short timeline allotted for the collection of evidence prior to the review, the team often met several times a week. The team collected documentary evidence from each campus for every criterion measure. Team members would return to their respective campuses, collect the campus evidence, and bring back their documentation to be archived in the notebooks that were created for the evaluators. Those documents that were aligned across the district proved most helpful in the collection process. Several large notebooks were developed to comprise all eight component areas for review by the evaluators to assist in their completion of the assessment process. This time together as a team also proved invaluable in developing strategies to assist students moving forward.

Challenges of the CAS Review Process for Academic Advising

TCCD's student support services greatly benefited from the CAS program review process, across many departments. Areas of improvement for the program review process in academic advising were also identified.

The quick timeline the institution placed on itself in an effort to be prepared for the SACSCOC review was the most challenging aspect of the program review process. Due to the fact that only one semester was allotted to complete the collection of evidence and assessment process—and this required the collaboration of five separate campuses—the endeavor proved difficult. Five campus directors and two academic advisors spent approximately 8 to 10 hours each week on CAS. It was a challenge to gather documents from all five campuses

(TCC Connect, TCCD's newest campus, had not yet been established at the time of this review) for every criterion measure. Although the academic advising offices are very similar in scope and function, how things are carried out varied for each campus. The redundancy of the various criterion measures was a challenge as well. Because the external evaluators were not familiar with academic advising at TCCD, many areas required additional narratives to fully inform the evaluators. In order to limit bias in evaluator rating, TCCD elected to use external evaluators with no connection to the functional area; although this was effective for that purpose, it also contributed to a lack of understanding of functional area practices and processes.

While such urgency on the part of TCCD led to many functional areas being assessed in a short period of time, it is recommended that a full academic year be allocated to complete each assessment process. An amazing amount of time and energy is expended in the collection of the evidence in preparation for the assessment; however, this only kicks off the work that is to come later.

If given the time, we would recommend a refined schedule that includes an initial semester dedicated to planning and gathering documentation. The following semester could involve the work of the external evaluators and the development of the functional area action plan(s). Subsequent semesters could be utilized to focus on the implementation and operationalization of the action plan(s). The program review process can be extremely effective in evaluating support and services to students; however, an assessment process can be quickly sabotaged if a team is too hasty or rushed to the point that it affects the thoroughness of the collection of evidence or the thoughtfulness of the development of an action plan.

Another challenge the directors of academic advising identified was based on the criterion measures of assessment by the evaluators. Often the criterion measures were beyond the directors' control. For example, the directors do not have control over the college website, nor do they have any say in the number of academic advisors and support staff. While the results of the assessment can be used to request changes, it was still a challenge to be rated low on items that were already known to be deficits. Therefore, creating an action plan to correct these areas was not always very realistic, given that the directors do not always determine resource allocation as part of the budget process for TCCD. This did, however, allow greater opportunity for the directors of academic advising to present these challenges and make a case with the campus vice presidents for student development services and administration collectively.

LESSONS LEARNED

The CAS program review process presented an opportunity to positively affect our institution. It provided a rich context for discussions based on the evaluator findings and action plan development. The collaborative approach of the functional areas—bringing campus leaders together to evaluate district and campus practices and processes—opened the door to sharing, innovation, and ingenuity.

Additionally, there were many takeaways from the CAS program review process. The accelerated rate at which this assessment was conducted provided an opportunity for the many areas of student development services to participate in the CAS review process—which was extremely beneficial for the Student Development Services Division—while, conversely, it challenged and exhausted many of the personnel participating in the process. A suggestion for future program review cycles is to begin 1 year in advance and create electronic folders related to the component areas. Additionally, one should not underestimate the role technology can play in the archival and compilation processes for documentation; technology should be harnessed to leverage efforts.

If the college has multiple campuses, every campus should save documents within the same system and save the documents by coding them by the CAS numbering system. If the college does not have a shared system, consider using a common site (e.g., DropBox, Google Docs, SharePoint) so that every campus can view all documents. Finally, teams should set timelines for reviewing the documents and make changes before the beginning of the next program review cycle, based on its formative assessment and summative evaluation.

A way to get ahead of the CAS review process is to identify areas that may be weak and strive to strengthen them before the process begins. With multiple campuses, work on consistency in programs, procedures, and documents. If at all possible, avoid having the same personnel involved in assessing two functional areas in back-to-back cycle periods. Also be mindful of "program review fatigue," as it may have a negative impact on the second assessment process.

Like every good student support services team, a program review team should be comprised of individuals with varying strengths—and put these strengths to work! For example, you might ask a colleague who is a technology guru to create the final presentation and product—substance is important, but never underestimate the benefit of an organized and pleasing presentation. Furthermore, it is important to identify a historian in the group. This person can assist in archiving information and evidence well before it is time to gather this information for a program review. A well-defined and organized clearinghouse can save your team hours of time, not to mention a great deal of frustration. Invite individuals on your team who have strategic thinking strengths and are good planners. They can help keep the CAS program review process in mind when moving through the whirlwind of everyday operations in your functional area. Identifying these roles for team members can be a lifesaver in your next review cycle.

If and when considering external evaluators, strive to find colleagues in comparable positions at similar colleges. The more the external reviewers know about the functional area at a similar institution, the more meaningful the evaluations can be for your functional area. For example, a director of continuing education may be an expert in her area and very effective in her job; however, she may have a difficult time evaluating an area that is outside of her purview. It would be better to involve someone who has a working knowledge of that functional area but who is not intimately involved with the parties and departments being assessed.

DEVELOPING THE ACTION PLAN

The CAS program review process is a valuable tool for evaluating programs in a structured and objective manner. It allows one to stop and take the time to critically examine programs and identify gaps in services. Since this assessment process, many new interventions have been initiated for students and many needed resources have been procured for TCCD. Some include required visits with an academic advisor for FTIC students, advisor manual registration for FTIC students, career-centric advisement, online new student group advisement, the addition of five online advisors for the district, the addition of student success coaches for our campuses, the addition of Vet Success counselors to be shared among our campuses through Veterans Affairs, and the addition of veterans' counselors at each campus.

For TCCD with five (at the time) distinct campuses, using the CAS standards for program review provided the impetus to establish consistency and standardization in academic advising practices across the district. Further, it instigated meaningful dialogue about what mattered most for student success through academic advising. Likely, one of the greatest outcomes of the use of the CAS standards in academic advising was the collaboration that occurred among the five directors of academic advising. While collaboration among these campus leaders is commonplace, a comprehensive program review at this level required deeper introspection across the units—something that had seldom been done with this level of thoroughness. As a result of the action plan and the work done throughout the entire CAS program review process, academic advising has established many student success initiatives that have greatly contributed to student success.

CONCLUSION

In summary, when TCCD sought a reliable tool for the assessment of its student development services area, it turned to the CAS standards. The CAS standards and approach assisted TCCD in meeting its goals in assessing student programs and services for compliance with SACSCOC Requirement 2.10 and Goal 3 of TCCD's Vision 2015 Strategic Plan. Moreover, it provided an educational experience for all participants—one that will not soon be forgotten. Program review teams celebrated their successes, discussed opportunities for growth and improvement, and collaborated about how to get the work done. Leaders emerged, and in the end TCCD became a better place for students.

REFERENCES

American Association of Community Colleges. (2016, February). Fast facts from our fact sheet. Retrieved from http://www.aacc.nche.edu/AboutCC/Pages/fastfactsfactsheet.aspx

Council for the Advancement of Standards in Higher Education. (2009). *Self-assessment guide: Academic advising.* Washington, DC: Author.

Council for the Advancement of Standards in Higher Education. (2015). *CAS professional standards for higher education* (9th ed.). Washington, DC: Author.

National Center for Education Statistics. (2015). *Total 12-month enrollment in degree-granting postsecondary institutions, by control and level of institution and state or jurisdiction: 2011-2012 and 2012-2013* [Data set]. Retrieved from https://nces.ed.gov/programs/digest/d14/tables/dt14_308.10.asp

Southern Association of Colleges and Schools Commission on Colleges. (2009). *The principles of accreditation: Foundations for quality enhancement.* Retrieved from http://www.sacscoc.org/pdf/2010principlesofacreditation.pdf

Chapter 7

Using the CAS Standards at a Multicampus Institution
The Arkansas State University–Beebe Story

Deborah Garrett and David Mayes

Assessment-driven program reviews at institutions with multiple campus locations require a strategic approach to develop a process that is inclusive of each campus location. At Arkansas State University–Beebe (ASU–Beebe), our experience has provided insights into successfully conducting program reviews using the standards established by the Council for the Advancement of Standards in Higher Education (CAS) at a multicampus institution, including designing the program, incorporating student learning and program outcomes, strategically selecting the review team, training the review team, assessing the role of each campus location, addressing the challenges associated with multiple campus locations, and compiling results and writing action plans for continual improvement of each campus site.

ASU–BEEBE

ASU–Beebe is a unique institution. As a 2-year university with four campuses and multiple sites (such as local high schools and industrial locations, as defined by the Higher Learning Commission), our institution has programs and services not found at any other 2-year (and some 4-year) institutions in the state of Arkansas. By state law, ASU–Beebe is the only 2-year institution that is allowed to have residence halls and a residence life program. This is critical to the institution's success, because of the rare programs that have statewide or regional missions. Some of those programs include agriculture equipment technology (John Deere technology), veterinary technology, and pharmacy technology.

As varied as the academic programs, the student body includes students of diverse ages and backgrounds: some are full time and others part time; some are employed, and some are underemployed; some are current active duty military students and dependents enrolled at the Little Rock Air Force Base site. At present, students come from 60 out of 75 counties in the state of Arkansas, 35 states, and a dozen other countries.

As with other multicampus institutions, our system faces the challenge of providing meaningful and consistent learning experiences through programs and services that meet the unique needs of each student population and community that ASU–Beebe serves. The total enrollment for the ASU–Beebe system is approximately 4,000 students. About half of the students are enrolled at the Beebe campus. Delivering appropriate experiences at each of the smaller campuses and determining the best ways to serve those respective communities requires intentional effort.

BACKGROUND

In August 2008, Deborah Garrett began as the new vice chancellor for student services and quickly learned of an approaching self-study and visit by an accreditation team. To prepare for the visit, Garrett decided to implement assessment processes in order to demonstrate effectiveness of the programs (Schuh & Upcraft, 2001). One of her first tasks was to review the assessment efforts currently in progress by the many functional areas within the student services division.

Garrett discovered that the division had an incomplete approach to assessment and a lack of data or evidence to make sound decisions. She challenged the student services leadership team to consult with national organizations and colleagues to learn more about best practices. The team returned with the recommendation to use the CAS standards and Self-Assessment Guides (SAGs) as the formal program review process.

Unfortunately, the first attempts to conduct CAS program reviews at ASU–Beebe failed. There continued to be a lack of data and evidence, and many members of the leadership team felt threatened by the consequences of the assessment revealing disappointing results (Suskie, 2009). Because of a lack of experience with the process, the leadership team had to grow to trust and understand that the purpose of assessment was to continually improve programs and thereby increase student success.

In the early implementation of using the CAS standards, ASU–Beebe only reviewed 7 of the 12 subsections of the standards (see Chapter 1). As each review team made initial and follow-up reports to the leadership team, the support and feedback from colleagues allowed the group to develop competence in conducting accurate program reviews. This competence helped the leadership team gain confidence in conducting program reviews, allowing for all parts of the standards to be used in assessing student services programs.

DESIGNING THE PROGRAM

The student services leadership team began meeting monthly in 2008 to discuss the implementation of systematic assessment using the

CAS standards. The meetings were conducted on all of the campus locations and included the directors from each of the student services departments, key members from each campus location, and invited guests. The group averaged about 15 directors, executive directors, and a vice chancellor at each meeting. A proposed agenda was distributed in advance to each member of the leadership team, with an invitation to add items to the agenda.

During the developmental phase, the CAS program review process at ASU–Beebe was shared with colleagues from academic affairs at annual collaborative retreats. Faculty members were also included on committees and student services task forces (Culp & Dungy, 2012). This collaborative effort resulted in greater institutional support.

The initial meetings served to develop—across the institution—collaborative relationships that encouraged involvement and feedback by key institutional stakeholders. This approach was used to allow institutional leaders to conceptualize and buy into the assessment process.

The assessment process for student affairs programs should be an ongoing organizational practice relevant for institutional policymaking (Keeling, Wall, Underhile, & Dungy, 2008), and it should include leaders from all across campus in order to encourage buy-in and support. The ASU–Beebe leadership team developed a comprehensive list of the functional areas for CAS program reviews and a 5-year assessment cycle to conduct the ongoing reviews. Figure 7.1 shows the 5-year program review cycle, and the steps are further explained throughout this chapter.

Figure 7.1. **The 5-Year Program Review Cycle**

Year 1	• Determine student learning outcomes and program outcomes to be assessed that are consistent with the CAS standards and that are appropriate for the institution's student populations. • Begin to assess and collect data.
Year 2	• Continue to assess and collect data.
Year 3	• Prepare for the CAS program review process. • Analyze data collected from prior 2 years and conduct ratings. • Develop action plan for improvement. • Write initial report.
Year 4	• Present report and action plans. • Begin to implement changes.
Year 5	• Continue to implement action plans. • Develop final report: 　• Prepare descriptive report of changes implemented. 　• Describe impact of changes. 　• List those changes yet to be implemented and justifications. • Develop student learning outcomes and program outcomes for the next cycle. • Present report to team and/or supervisor.

INCORPORATING STUDENT LEARNING AND PROGRAM OUTCOMES

Student learning outcomes are essential to establish clear expectations of what students should learn by participating in a program (Timm, Davis-Barham, McKinney, & Knerr, 2013). At ASU–Beebe, our development and refinement of intended student learning and program outcomes has been an ongoing process.

The initial student learning outcomes were developed by the student services leadership team at an off-site retreat. These outcomes allowed the student services division's leadership team to transition from assessing satisfaction to assessing student learning and development (Bresciani, Zelna, & Anderson, 2004).

The ASU–Beebe intended learning outcomes were then shared and modified at collaborative academic affairs and student services retreats. The next challenge was for each department within student services to develop specific desired learning outcomes to be assessed each year. In the current system, progress in assessing the learning outcomes is reviewed each year, and modifications to programs and services are made as needed.

SELECTING THE REVIEW TEAM

The selection of the review team is a critical consideration for multicampus institutions. One of the first steps in establishing a review team is determining who will be in its leadership. At ASU–Beebe, the chair of the review team, as it is established every 5 years, is appointed by the vice chancellor for student services. The chair recommends the review team members to the vice chancellor for student services with a rationale for inclusion. The members of the review team serve on the team until the ratings have been conducted and the initial report has been completed.

The review team includes key personnel from each campus location as well as individuals with expertise in the subject matter. The chair determines who is most important in the review team's success when selecting members of the review team. Team members are selected based on a variety of criteria and considered based on whether the prospective team member will develop a sense of belonging for each campus location, help control for bias in the rating of a functional area, and work together with other team members to develop agreement with organization objectives based on the CAS standards.

The number of raters is determined by maximum efficiency and effectiveness: The review team should be large enough to achieve a comprehensive review, but small enough to accomplish the program review in a timely manner. Review teams are inclusive of perspectives from all campus locations, have personnel with expertise in the subject area, and include student voices. The average size of the review teams at ASU–Beebe is five individuals.

Garrett encourages the use of faculty members on review teams in a collaborative process (Yousey-Elsener, Bentrim, & Henning, 2015). Their inclusion in assessment helps to promote the development of a culture of evidence at the institution (Culp & Dungy, 2012). In addition, the CAS review process helps to build collaborative relationships across the institution.

CAS review teams also include expert external reviewers who bring unbiased perspectives from outside of the institution and ask questions that might not be obvious to internal reviewers. The selection of external reviewers is based on knowledge in the field of study, availability at the time of the review, and willingness to participate.

One additional consideration is whether all campus locations have the program being reviewed. For example, at Arkansas State University, the only campus location that has residence halls is the Beebe campus. The review team for housing and residence life included employees from residence life, an on-campus student, someone from the maintenance department, and an expert from another institution; however, each campus location has admissions staff. So, the admissions review team included an employee from each campus location and an admissions director from another 2-year college in Arkansas.

TRAINING THE REVIEW TEAM

It is essential to train the review team prior to conducting a program review. Furthermore, in order to create a culture of assessment, team members must champion the cause (Yousey-Elsener et al., 2015). At ASU–Beebe, the vice chancellor for student services has conducted several training workshops for program review teams. The purposes of these trainings are to educate the review teams on assessment and to foster a culture of assessment. As members of the student services leadership have gained expertise, the experienced directors have conducted review team trainings with other staff. Training begins with identifying the overall process that will be used to educate the team on the program review process. This includes describing the meetings or training programs that will be needed, identifying a facilitator for trainings, and developing a training agenda.

Training programs also include a description of how to rate a standard. Typically, the review team engages in discussion on how to judge performance on a criterion. Criterion measures are designed to be evaluated using a scale ranging from insufficient evidence to exemplary. Prior to conducting a program review, it is important for each rating committee to discuss the evidence needed to arrive at a conclusion on how well a criterion is met.

COMPILING RESULTS AND WRITING AN ACTION PLAN

After the review team finishes the ratings, the initial report is prepared by the team leader. This report gives an executive summary of the process, a listing of team members, the functional area ratings, answers to the discussion questions at the end of each section of the SAG, action plans to address weaknesses, and any additional comments about the evaluation. The report is prepared, distributed, and verbally presented to the members of the student services leadership team during one of the monthly meetings. The members of the leadership team are encouraged to give feedback about each program review, the results, and recommendations for improvement of action plans. Because of active participation in the process, members of the leadership team have developed more confidence and competence in performing program reviews. At this point, frequent questions arise about the data and evidence provided by each campus and about conclusions on the next steps in moving forward.

Every 6 months, the team leader returns to the student services leadership team to give an update on the progress toward completing the action plan. This cycle continues until the action plan is complete. At that time, a final report is prepared by the review team and sent to the office of the vice chancellor for student services.

As members of the leadership team have changed at ASU–Beebe, it has been necessary to alter the schedule of the assessment cycle. These alterations have allowed for the division to adjust to the challenges of each functional area. Because many of the directors on the leadership team are responsible for several functional areas, it has been important to prioritize the assessment needs for the student affairs division.

Once a review cycle has been completed, the process starts over with a new program review for that functional area. To continually improve each functional area, the goal is to conduct a program review for each functional area once in each five-year cycle. Additionally, each functional area assesses intended program and learning outcomes each academic year.

A challenge for us has been importing our reports into the university's assessment tracking system. The current system does not allow for the entire report to be uploaded with all the data and evidence attached. Each section of the standards, SAGs, and ratings have to be uploaded separately, which does not allow for the review of just one comprehensive document. Because several cycles of program reviews had been completed while preparing for our accreditation self-study, the reports became part of the electronic evidence file for the visiting team.

CHALLENGES WITH IMPLEMENTATION

Our student services leadership team identified several challenges involved in conducting CAS program reviews for a multicampus institution. One obvious challenge is considering the uniqueness of each campus while assessing the functional area. In many cases, the standard is met on one or more campuses but not at other locations. Accurately assessing and reporting the findings has evolved as members of the leadership team have gained experience in program reviews.

Appreciating the different campus environments and different students can be challenging in applying a standard consistently. The leadership team found that the assessments often focused too much on the campus with the largest enrollment. By focusing on purposeful inclusion of each campus location, the leadership team began to conduct program reviews that took into account the uniqueness of each campus location.

Reflecting on who is served at a campus location and how is critical in making decisions. For example, the Beebe and Heber Springs campuses have full-scale dining operations. The Searcy campus has a smaller operation, and the Little Rock Air Force Base does not have a dining operation. In the rating of dining services, it was critical to first define the scope of the operation on each campus in order to have a usable end product. Because of staff who are responsible for programs and services at each campus, the rating team attempted to have one score that represented the function across all of the campuses—but differences in scope and size of the operation have not always allowed us to do so.

Another challenge has been coordinating the rating team's schedules. Synchronizing travel schedules, where to meet, and training needs of the team have to be taken into account. The logistics of including raters from different locations has posed several challenges; however, inclusion of all campus locations is critical to long-term success and assessment efforts at each campus location.

REFLECTIONS FROM PROGRAM REVIEWS

The student services division was first to develop and adopt general student learning outcomes that were mapped across the division at ASU–Beebe. Those initial intended outcomes have since been adopted by the university.

In addition to the information gleaned regarding student learning and achieved program outcomes in individual functional areas, there were unanticipated gains as a result of using the CAS standards and the recommended review process. Because of the approach taken in developing the rating teams (considering those most important to the success of the functional areas across the institution), student services has developed more advocates, both internally and externally, through cross-functional collaboration.

As the student services leadership team learned from CAS program reviews, the review team was able to identify specific professional development needs for the entire division. The identification of professional development needs has been foundational in providing in-service workshops during the quarterly all-staff student services meetings.

Another unanticipated outcome has been an enhanced commitment to assessment and student development across the student services division. Through the work of creating measurable student learning and program outcomes, the student services leadership team has learned to consistently reflect on what students are learning in ASU–Beebe cocurricular programs.

CONCLUSION

Student learning takes place as students are engaged in educationally purposeful programs outside of the classroom (Bresciani et al., 2004; Keeling et al., 2008; Schuh & Upcraft, 2001; Timm et al., 2013).

Multiple campus systems pose different challenges in assessing that learning, but the ASU–Beebe leadership team has led the university forward in implementing an ongoing CAS program review process that continues to benefit all campuses and improve collaboration across divisions. Additionally, by working together as a team, collaborating with faculty members, and continually evaluating programs, the student services division has become more united around a common purpose.

REFERENCES

Bresciani, M. J., Zelna, C. L., & Anderson, J. A. (2004). *Assessing student learning and development: A handbook for practitioners.* Washington, DC: National Association of Student Personnel Administrators.

Culp, M. M., & Dungy, G. J. (2012). *Building a culture of evidence in student affairs: A guide for leaders and practitioners.* Washington, DC: National Association of Student Personnel Administrators.

Keeling, R. P., Wall, A. F., Underhile, R., & Dungy, G. J. (2008). *Assessment reconsidered: Institutional effectiveness for student success.* Washington, DC: International Center for Student Success and Institutional Accountability.

Schuh, J. H., & Upcraft, M. L. (2001). *Assessment practice in student affairs: An applications manual.* San Francisco, CA: Jossey-Bass.

Suskie, L. A. (2009). *Assessing student learning: A common sense guide.* San Francisco, CA: Jossey-Bass.

Timm, D. K., Davis-Barham, J., McKinney, K., & Knerr, A. R. (2013). *Assessment in practice: A companion guide to the ASK standards.* Washington, DC: American College Personnel Association.

Yousey-Elsener, K., Bentrim, E. M., & Henning, G. W. (2015). *Coordinating student affairs divisional assessment: A practical guide.* Sterling, VA: Stylus.

Chapter 8

Using the CAS Standards in Housing and Residence Life
Lessons From a Small Private Institution

Dave Rozeboom

"Campus atmosphere and especially residential living arrangements are crucial [for student development and transformation]" (Light, 2001, p. 10). I have led assessment efforts at multiple institutions, and I have been directly involved in leading housing-related and residence life programs at Baylor University (BU), St. Edward's University (SEU), and Hardin-Simmons University (HSU), where I used the standards established by the Council for the Advancement of Standards in Higher Education (CAS). Although all three are private institutions, they represent the spectrum of private institutions in size as Division I, II, and III schools, respectively. Yet size differences aside, each institution has had to make changes in order to stay relevant. These adjustments have been informed by assessments, which have helped to improve institutional effectiveness. At all three schools, CAS provided a framework with which to inform these assessments.

This chapter looks closely at why assessment—particularly one that is guided by the CAS standards—is important in housing and residence life, with attention given to students, the institution, student affairs division, and student affairs professionals. In exploring the *why*, *who*, and *how* of assessment in residence life, we participate in an effort to gather, analyze, and interpret evidence, which in turn sheds light on institutional, divisional, or agency effectiveness (Upcraft & Schuh, 1996). This leads to recommendations, benefits, and challenges of doing this particular work, but the granular movement from purpose to practice illustrates the incredible value such an undertaking can deliver.

THE WHY

The purpose for assessment in housing and residence life is clear: Residence life is critical in the university's mission to foster student engagement, persistence, and success, and in order to meet these outcomes, we must seek continuous improvement. The first priority of the residence life professional is student success. In the book *Surviving to Thriving*, Soliday and Mann (2013) quoted Joretta Nelson addressing student success in terms of transformation and development: "Thriving private institutions are placing student success at the center of their focus" (p. 136). Furthermore, learning outside of traditional academia, especially in residential settings and activities, is vital to the holistic success of students (Light, 2001). As institutional leaders, we must be committed to students' success and seek avenues for continuous improvement. I have witnessed CAS nudge residence life areas to be better; in fact, CAS was actually established in order to champion student learning and development (CAS, 2009). Most recently, I have utilized the CAS approach in order to drive continuous improvement at HSU, beginning with the development of mission statements for each of its units.

It is important to see the critical role the CAS standards play in the big picture of assessment. I have found that similar to good theory, good assessment provides a frame of reference, serves as a mode of analysis, and, ultimately, can and should be used to guide good decision making. Assessment helps answer many questions that range from the quality of programs to alignment with institutional mission, to cost-effectiveness. "Assessment in student affairs is no longer a 'luxury' that is done only after all other priorities have been taken care of. Assessment is now a necessity that demands our highest priority" (Upcraft & Schuh, 1996, p. 323). In terms of benchmarking, assessments like the National Survey of Student Engagement—or, for residence life, Educational Benchmarking, Inc. (EBI), become invaluable; however, the beauty of the CAS standards is that they provide a thorough framework for self-assessment along the way.

Assessment in residence life helps highlight concerns with student satisfaction and inclusivity, institutional effectiveness, tracking progress toward excellence, and student learning. Professionals in residence life understand why dormitories (from the Latin *dormir*, "to sleep") often miss the point when it comes to learning because, void of intentional programming and organizational structure, residence halls are indeed simply a place to sleep. Enhancing student learning and development does not occur automatically; rather, a responsibility remains to create "intentional, planned, and structured learning experiences [for student engagement]" (Kerr & Tweedy, 2006, p. 11). Thus, the housing and residence life program (and all that it entails) must be intentional about both learning as well as the environment that fosters it; assessing program effectiveness is fitting.

Indeed, are such *conditions* being created? Are students satisfied with their living and learning *experience*? Measurable learning objectives provide a targeted approach to examining the efficacy of learning programs. Astin's (1991) I-E-O model (inputs, environment, and outputs) is often used as an assessment framework for housing and

residence life, particularly because it "reflects the fundamental rationale for living–learning programs: that through developing them, the
institution structures the environment in such a way that the students
are affected in intentional and desirable ways" (Dunn & Dean, 2013,
p. 17). Yet housing and residence life has many components that have
an impact on learning, albeit sometimes indirectly, and therein lies the
value of CAS standards: identifying how each component affects the
student experience.

THE WHO AND THE WHAT

When using the CAS standards to conduct assessments of existing
programs and services, an important part of the process is developing a review team. *Who* does the assessment, and *what* does a CAS
assessment of housing and residence life look like? You need professionals who are committed to confronting the brutal facts—in other
words, people willing to look at current operating conditions and
identify room for growth, no matter how spacious (Collins, 2001).
My use of the CAS standards in all of my work has shed light on
areas that need growth. In essence, the CAS standards are best used
when there is a willingness to confront the brutal facts, because
by doing so, improvements can be made. Moving forward with
assessment starts with developing the team willing to expose gaps
and work toward creating better opportunities for student growth
and development.

A clearly defined purpose and direction is crucial: If the right people
are not involved, the project will lag or falter altogether. One of the critical aspects of a self-assessment is the selection and preparation of the
self-assessment review team. In addition to residence life, I employed
the CAS standards as part of the divisional assessment at BU in 2006.
That particular team was made up of about 12 individuals who were

not only a diverse representation of the division but also willing to critically examine our operations in light of best practice. The leadership of the vice president—now a president at a sister institution—was crucial, as he clearly thought strategically about that team and, as a result, set up the assessment process for success.

At SEU in 2008, our residence life leadership team was the review team, primarily because we felt that an internal review was necessary. That leadership team was made up of the director and three associate directors of residence life, who had diverse areas of expertise. Although some strong assessment practices had been in place for a number of years, using the CAS standards helped us better understand and improve our operations.

At HSU in 2013, a smaller private institution, a position was created from the already established sustainability position dedicated to leading assessment efforts. That position (coordinator for assessment, sustainability, and academic success) changed again after the completion of the review. It may seem counterintuitive to have so much thrown into one job description; however, it is often the case that smaller institutions have more needs than there are personnel to fulfill them, requiring leadership to add to a team member's job description in order to maintain momentum.

Suffice it to say, the choice of leadership for the CAS program review process may differ by institution, yet the decision to engage the process requires commitment from senior leadership. Ideally, "champions" are designated to ensure the assessment's completion, but ultimately the responsibility for assessment rests at the organizational apex. This commitment is measured by the dedication of both time and training—which depend on structured deadlines and well-chosen team members. Each of the aforementioned institutions made clear the desire for and necessity of the assessment: It was something that was needed "yesterday." The process at BU took about a year, but our committee's leaders had experience in using the CAS standards in other areas. We spent a number of hours collectively walking through the various domains and dimensions for the purpose of prioritizing our observations. In those meetings we were provided with pages upon pages of documents that had already been collected and would aid our effort. I vividly recall the leader, well-versed in the CAS standards, walking us through each of the areas we would subsequently assess.

Contrast that process with the CAS program review process at the two smaller institutions. At SEU, the leadership took a "divide and conquer" approach, dedicating a few resident directors to take on the bulk of the effort as one of their "collateral" assignments. They were selected for their skill sets but also because they had the least challenging of the residence halls in terms of day-to-day task and behavior management, providing them more opportunity to invest in the review. BU provided in-depth training, whereas the training at SEU meant simply handing over the latest edition of the CAS standards. Similarly, at HSU, resources were provided with the directive to self-instruct. I would not deem those latter examples as best practices, but unfortunately they are typical at smaller institutions.

An important aspect of training is helping a team understand the General Standards. The CAS standards include areas for review in housing and residence life programs. "When used for self-assessment and program review, each functional area standard (with the embedded General Standards) provides criteria by which leaders in an institution and functional area can judge the quality and effectiveness of current educational efforts" (CAS, 2015, p. 27). It is worth noting that a cursory approach to all of the components can yield results, but thoroughly dissecting them individually will yield the most improvement.

THE HOW

Now that we have a good understanding of the *why*, *who*, and *what*, let us examine *how* the process works. At HSU, we used the CAS standards at both the division and department levels, with the collection of materials better in some areas than others. Compiling documentation is an important but challenging part of the assessment process; sometimes there is a lack of documentation (nothing on the website, a lack of forms, etc.), or there is a lack of competence while gathering documentation. Both challenges slow down the assessment process.

Gathering documentation can reveal much anecdotally about the commitment to continuous improvement in an area. The application of the CAS standards was different for HSU than it was for SEU. Listed below are specific examples from each of the areas at the two smaller private institutions for which documents were reviewed.

Mission

At SEU, a residence life mission statement was in existence prior to the self-assessment process, so the assessment examined the alignment of this mission with the division and university as well as whether it still captured what we believed we were trying to accomplish. HSU did not have a mission statement for residence life, and thus we were aware that more effort would be required in articulating the mission. What also made it more challenging was the lack of a divisional mission statement.

Program

"As residence education, student affairs, and housing professionals, our message that 'residential' and 'learning' are a single idea—residential learning—is paramount" (Shushok, Scales, Sriram, & Kidd, 2011, p. 20). The program review is quite dependent upon the established student learning and development outcomes. SEU already had some learning

outcomes established for its living–learning communities. As with the
mission, the work was going to be in the review of the existing learning outcomes and the room available for program improvement. This
examination included an in-depth look at our programming model
and its effectiveness, particularly in light of the profession's movement
from the wellness wheel to mission-centered conversations. SEU was
also at a point to collect information on the student learning and development domains and dimensions. In collecting that information—
some of which came from the newly formed Global Understanding
and Social Justice Living–Learning Communities—we were able to
see the particular strides that had already been made in regard to the
civic engagement domain. When we began the process of looking for
established outcomes at HSU, we found that no particular student outcomes had been established—and not just for residence life, but for the
entire division of student affairs.

Organization and Leadership

Both SEU and HSU already had strategic planning documentation
for housing and residence life, yet it became quite apparent that both
were in need of a strategic plan beyond the goals, objectives, and planned
assessments. Though organizational charts, performance expectations,
policies and procedures, and goals existed, the CAS program review
process helped to illustrate the needed growth in those organizational
components. For example, SEU had many documented policies and
procedures. One that came to be reviewed more fully as a result of the
CAS assessment was our alcohol poisoning hospital and EMS protocol.
Professional development as part of management and supervision was
also available, but more attention was needed for professional development plans that would encourage and support scholarly contributions
to the profession.

One component of the program advancement subsection of the

General Standards (CAS, 2015) includes incorporating sustainability practices in the management and design of programs, services, and facilities. The CAS program review process showed that residence life at HSU had indeed made strides to articulate sustainability efforts as part of the year-end reporting, even though other organizational and leadership areas were lacking.

One of the subpoints under the strategic planning subsection of the General Standards (CAS, 2015) speaks to engagement in addition to promoting environments that provide opportunities for student learning and development. At BU, we examined the residence halls and actually found signage in one building that was heavily using "not" and "no" language, indicating a closed environment rather than one open for student engagement. This examination led to changes to this living and learning environment.

Human Resources

Some of the documents collected for this area at SEU were internally generated, such as the organizational charts and operational plans. Other documents primarily came from the human resources office, including but not limited to the performance enhancement program, workshops and seminars for supervisors, the background check consent form, the SEU operating principles, and the SEU hiring guidelines. In essence, SEU had solid documentation to review this particular component. A similar examination of documentation at HSU found that many policies, procedures, and protocols were understood only by word of mouth.

Ethics

At SEU, the relevant documentation included language regarding confidentiality, appropriate use of institutional funds, and expectations for behavior. Documents with such language included job descriptions and divisional expectations. Not surprisingly, much of the ethics piece seemed to be taken for granted at HSU, although there were some documents containing similar language.

Law, Policy, and Governance

Even though SEU had a risk management office, and the human resources director at HSU also wore the "safety director" hat, both residence life programs needed to examine programs and services for risks, liabilities, and limitations. Specifically, the CAS program review process helped SEU realize that policy was needed for the newest residence hall, as its construction created a potential "climbing wall" hazard. HSU's use of the CAS standards made it very clear that there was a larger gap in terms of policies and foreseeable legal challenges with such things as residence hall evacuation.

Diversity, Equity, and Access

Although SEU had already been recognized as a Hispanic-serving institution and boasted a strong international program, residence life looked closely at the inclusivity of language and pictures in various documents and how selection and training of resident assistants (RAs) addressed this area. The use of the CAS standards at HSU ultimately helped to address necessary changes in unintentional lack of access to RA positions for students of color.

Internal and External Relations

Divisional meetings and agendas typically demonstrated the opportunity for residence life to share information with other departments. At both SEU and HSU, the development of collaborative practices with admissions, the registrar, athletics, and other constituencies became quite apparent throughout the year—and in particular during the orientation process. Sometimes such collaboration was illustrated by special committee agendas and minutes, such as the housing task force and the "servicescape" committees at SEU.

Financial Resources

At SEU, documents compiled included the hiring guidelines and job descriptions for positions in residence life (from human resources), the financial guidelines from the division, and the printouts of cost center utilization (budget management). At both SEU and HSU, programming dollars per individual student was calculated in order to demonstrate unmet need and to make the case for new programs and services.

Technology

Surveys like EBI became very valuable at both SEU and HSU in illustrating the need for better technology, particularly in relation to customer service in the housing assignments process. The CAS review of technology helped both institutions transition to better housing management platforms.

Facilities and Equipment

At both SEU and HSU, the examination of adequate study space resulted in changes. At SEU, creating a list of spaces and their uses helped with gaining a better understanding of the facilities. The CAS program review process also led to the examination of mattress and technology rotation, computer lab usage, laundry accessibility, and the placement of fire and safety signage, lighting, etc.

Assessment

At SEU, the senior associate director did a phenomenal job of creating a grid that listed all of the programmatic areas within residence life and whether those areas had corresponding assessment plans. For example, she found that the Living Learning Community programs did have evaluative components, but that the RAs did not have periodic job performance reviews. The collection of such data helped division leadership to pinpoint which programs and functions needed assessment. At HSU, assessment within residence life was virtually nonexistent.

While these illustrations are by no means exhaustive, they serve to underscore why documentation is critical to the change management process. The differentiation in documentation by institution is necessary to show that the starting points for improvement were vastly different.

ASSIGNING RATINGS

The next part of the CAS process for program review is assigning ratings. Collecting data is one thing; assigning ratings to those data is another. The rating continuum we developed ranged from 1 to 5 in meeting the CAS criteria, where 1 signaled "did not meet"; 2 equated to "partly meets"; 3 stood for "meets"; 4 meant "exceeds"; and 5 equated to "exemplary." Ratings of "Does Not Apply (ND)" and "Insufficient Evidence/Unable To Rate (0)" could also be used. An institution that lacks documentation may decide to build the various areas rather than rating each of them, since such ratings would likely be 0 or 1. This documentation included forms and processes as well as surveys and evaluations. As mentioned earlier, individuals (or groups of people, as at BU) were assigned to examine the collected documentation and offer a rating, which was then reviewed (and adjusted as needed) by the review team.

Two specific examples from the finance section of residence life at SEU illuminate the ratings in action. Our team of reviewers gave a "Partly Met" score of 2 for the division being adequately funded to accomplish its mission and goals. One specific reason was the lack of dollars dedicated to strengthening the living–learning program. Other areas were underfunded but still seen as important to the university mission; they included faculty partner programs, transition programs, and more assessment. When assessing if funding priorities are determined with the context of program mission, student needs, and available resources, our reviewers scored a 4. Because the allocation of funds was directly linked to priorities, this area did not prove to be a gap that needed to be addressed.

Another example from SEU pertains to the section on human resources, with residence life meeting or exceeding standards in most of the sections and identifying areas of growth for others. Our review team found multiple gaps related to the human resources standards for residence life. We found that hiring flowcharts needed to be developed. We also found that we lacked evaluation and opportunities for continuing development for our student staff as well as promotion protocols for our professional staff. The review helped us realize that position descriptions needed to be reviewed and revised and tied to performance evaluation.

Another example comes from the assessment section of SEU's residence life program. The ratings were predominantly 2 or "Partly Meets." In terms of a "grand assessment strategy," we found that we did not have an overarching assessment strategy, but we did believe that we could further apply the university's existing data sets for decision making. Another finding was that residence life assessment criteria were rarely established before program implementation, and measurable outcomes were often not decided prior. In our review it also became clear that even though some aspects of residence life had intentionally developed student learning outcomes (such as RA class), this was not the case for most of our efforts. Ultimately, we came away with a common understanding that "assessment" was an area needing quite a bit of investment and improvement. As a result, we began to strengthen our assessment efforts by identifying outcomes prior to program implementation.

IMPLEMENTING CHANGE

The last component of the CAS program review process is the actual implementation of change. Implementing change involves clearly outlining what changes are to be made and the time frame with which to make them. Moving into implementation also involves sharing the information with appropriate constituencies. For example, if the financial section includes areas for improvement related to funding, the case must be made with those who can provide the funds. The review team should identify which constituencies need to review which data. It would make sense to share the residence life areas for improvement with the greater residence life team, particularly if the team will be involved in the continuous improvement process. The rated information and action items can also be used as leverage. For example, given the profession's understanding of living–learning programs as a high-impact practice (Kuh, 2008), sharing low program section data with divisional leadership and/or passionate faculty can help institute necessary change.

When I arrived at HSU, living–learning programs were a foreign concept. The utilization of the CAS standards, in conjunction with consultants, helped the campus better understand their purpose and necessity. Additionally, high-level reports were often made available to members of the institution's executive leadership team in order to educate them on the needs of student affairs. Such sharing can increase program credibility, provide a baseline for future assessment, and demonstrate commitment to continuous improvement.

Although I have shared some specific efforts with using the CAS standards, the following are a few benefit highlights:

- The comprehensive review can be used to illustrate the significant role that housing and residence life plays in the life of the university.
- Invariably, some aspect of needed improvement is identified; the results can provide the necessary leverage for change.
- Assessment preparation, documentation collection, and corresponding analysis promote professional development for staff and fosters collaboration.
- A commitment to implementing continuous improvement demonstrates to students and other constituencies that student success is paramount.

There are challenges with each stage of the journey, beginning with finding the right people to invest in this depth of understanding and continuing with deciding on a collection strategy, working through a timeline, coming to agreement regarding ratings, developing a reasonable action plan, and making changes. Understanding why assessment is important will drive engagement with the process, but wisely choosing who will provide leadership for collecting and rating the data can benefit efficiency. In my experience, the challenges were amplified in direct correlation with the smaller size of the institution, primarily because of the cross-functional nature of personnel.

Clearly, using the CAS standards in a program review is a process that requires intentionality, but ultimately it can be very rewarding for housing and residence life staff and stakeholders. "Since the primary goals of student affairs professionals are to facilitate students' development, to understand and design educationally purposeful environments, and to be experts about organizations and how they function, it is our responsibility, both professionally and ethically, to know and understand the individuals, groups, and institutions with whom we work" (Komives & Woodard, 2003, p. 154). The success of residence life professionals in fostering student engagement depends on the ability to seek continuous improvement, and employing the CAS standards furthers that effort. Ultimately, the desired result is sharing the data with appropriate constituencies and implementing the needed changes in residence life and housing to benefit student success through learning and development.

REFERENCES

Astin, A. W. (1991). *Assessment for excellence.* New York, NY: Macmillan.

Collins, J. (2001). *Good to great.* New York, NY: HarperCollins.

Council for the Advancement of Standards in Higher Education. (2009). *CAS professional standards for higher education* (7th ed.). Washington, DC: Author.

Council for the Advancement of Standards in Higher Education. (2015). *CAS professional standards for higher education* (9th ed.). Washington, DC: Author.

Dunn, M. S., & Dean, L. A. (2013). Together we can live and learn: Living-learning communities as integrated curricular experiences. *A Journal of Leisure Studies & Recreation Education, 28*(1), 11–23.

Kerr, K. G., & Tweedy, J. (2006). Beyond set time and student satisfaction: A curricular approach to residential education. *About Campus, 11*(5), 9–15.

Komives, S., & Woodard, D. (2003). *Student services: A handbook for the profession* (4th ed.). San Francisco, CA: Jossey-Bass.

Kuh, G. (2008). *High-impact educational practices: What they are, who has access to them, and why they matter.* Retrieved from http://provost.tufts.edu/celt/files/High-Impact-Ed-Practices1.pdf

Light, R. J. (2001). *Making the most of college: Students speak their minds.* Cambridge, MA: Harvard University Press.

Soliday, J., & Mann, R. (2013). *Surviving to thriving: A planning framework for leaders of private colleges & universities.* Whitsett, NC: Credo Press.

Shushok, F., Scales, T., Sriram, R., & Kidd, V. (2011). A tale of three campuses: Unearthing theories of residential life that shape the student learning experience. *About Campus, 16*(3), 13–21.

Upcraft, M. L., & Schuh, J. H. (1996). *Assessment in student affairs: A guide for practitioners.* San Francisco, CA: Jossey-Bass.

Chapter 9

Using the CAS Standards for LGBTQ Services
Examples from a Large Public Research Institution

Alex C. Lange

esbian, gay, bisexual, trans, and queer (LGBTQ) services and programs began to exist formally on college and university campuses in 1971 (Sanlo, 2000). As time has progressed, so have the forms and functions of these services, depending on their particular sociohistorical contexts. The purposes of LGBTQ centers and offices can include assessing and evaluating the campus climate for university community members, developing networks and services dedicated to supporting campus LGBTQ communities, providing and planning educational programs about LGBTQ communities, and advocating with and alongside LGBTQ student communities (Marine, 2011). To better support the unique needs and interests of those who work in gender and sexuality programs and services, the Consortium of Higher Education LGBT Resource Professionals was formed in 1997 (Marine, 2011); it is herein referred to as "the Consortium." LGBTQ services can be stand-alone offices and units or integrated into other

units—most often multicultural student services. With all of this varia-
tion in how LGBTQ services are administered and organized, there
is a great need to adhere to set standards to ensure consistency across
campuses and services; the standards established by the Council for
the Advancement of Standards in Higher Education (CAS) provide
several mechanisms to ensure this consistency.

This chapter discusses three of the ways in which I and others have
used both the CAS learning and development outcomes and the CAS
functional area–specific standards in LGBTQ programs and services,
which include: (1) development of learning outcomes, (2) benchmarking and institutional advocacy, and (3) Self-Assessment Guides
(SAGs). While most individuals and offices use the CAS standards to
conduct program reviews, there are other ways to think about using the
standards that can improve our impact on student learning and success.
More specifically, this chapter utilizes the lens of LGBTQ services to
describe how the functional area standards can be used in practice. Each
section discusses specific examples of my practice as well as particular
implications for others' use of the standards. As someone who has done
both community- and campus-based LGBTQ services work, I find the
CAS standards a key tool in my student affairs armamentarium.

DEVELOPING LEARNING OUTCOMES

Several foundational documents and texts in the student affairs literature continue to emphasize the role of student affairs professionals
as educators in the broader campus curriculum of the whole student,
assisting those with whom we work to become more intentional learners
(see, e.g., American College Personnel Association, 1994; CAS, 2015;
Keeling, 2004, 2006). Specifically, *Learning Reconsidered 2* calls for a
learning outcomes approach to guide the structure of our educational
strategies and interventions (Keeling, 2006). Indeed, being strategic and

intentional about student learning is one of the ways we can measure the impact of our programs and services on students (Harper, 2011).

The CAS standards assist student affairs educators in infusing intention and strategy into student learning. CAS (2015) identified six domains for student learning and development (see Appendix F for a complete list). Within each of these domains, particular examples of learning outcomes are offered as a way to allow for a more focused, intentional approach to learning, assessment, and evaluation (for examples, see CAS, 2015, p. 26).

Example in Practice: Developing Community Learning and Leadership Outcomes for LGBTQ Students

At Michigan State University (MSU), with a total enrollment of more than 50,000 students, we currently have 15 LGBTQ-centered organizations and collectives, each with varying purposes, funding, and structures. Though the MSU LGBT Resource Center has no formal oversight for any of the organizations, we continue to be tasked by administrators and students to engage LGBTQ student leaders and to cultivate a thriving on-campus LGBTQ community. To this end, the resource center developed a framework of community learning and leadership outcomes. To properly assess our impact on student learning, learning outcomes allow us to articulate the particular knowledge we hope students will gain from our programs and services across a variety of dimensions (e.g., factual, conceptual, procedural). In addition, our community learning and leadership outcomes also spanned from lower-order cognitive processes (e.g., remembering and understanding) to higher-order cognitive dimensions (e.g., evaluating and creating). This chapter does not discuss learning outcome design at length; instead, readers are encouraged to review Chapter 2 of this volume.

To develop these outcomes, we looked to two primary sources: the CAS learning and development outcomes as well as the institutional undergraduate learning goals. The CAS (2009) LGBT Programs and Services standards and guidelines assisted us in identifying the particular learning needs of LGBTQ students. These particular learning domains included realistic self-appraisal, self-understanding, and self-respect (intrapersonal development domain); identity development (intrapersonal development domain); and effective leadership (interpersonal competence domain). In addition to the CAS domains, we also used MSU's undergraduate learning goals to cross-reference how our outcome domains did or did not fit within institutional frameworks. For instance, one of the examples of the learning and development outcomes in the effective leadership dimension of CAS (2015) is to "communicate a vision, mission, or purpose that encourages commitment and action in others" (p. 29). Rather than just using this particular outcome, we've modified one of our community learning and leadership outcomes to be "articulate a vision of the MSU LGBTQ community that encourages care for one another and inclusion of all members" (Lange, 2015, p. 3). This outcome is also related to the MSU undergraduate learning goal focused on effective citizenship. This outcome is student-centered, focuses on the learning to be gained from an activity rather than focusing on the activity itself, and reflects the scaffolding of the institution and unit's missions and goals (L. Dean & A. Lange, webinar, January 26, 2015). The CAS learning and development outcomes provide language and frames of thinking about the intended learning demanded in the CAS LGBT Programs and Services standards and guidelines while also providing linkages to local frameworks for student learning and development (Komives & Smedick, 2012).

Challenges. Though the CAS learning and development outcomes provide a strong framework for thinking about learning outcome design for specific interventions, there have also been some challenges in meeting the standards set forth. For instance, our community learning and leadership outcomes still do not adequately address the humanitarianism and civic engagement domain. To address the whole student leader and the leader's complete engagement with the MSU LGBTQ community, more effort is needed in infusing global perspectives, social responsibility, and sense of civic responsibility outcomes into our student leader curriculum. However, we contribute to that particular domain through other intervention methods. Even though we would ideally like to have all the learning domains reflected in our framework, we still seek to address the needs of that domain elsewhere in the LGBT Resource Center's work.

In addition, not all staff members possess the same knowledge and familiarity with using the CAS learning and development outcomes in practice, making it difficult to come to common understandings and implementations of intended learning outcomes across programs and services. More attention is being given so that all staff members can have similar understandings as to why and how we use the CAS standards in our practice.

Takeaways for Developing Learning Outcomes

The CAS learning and development outcome domains allow practitioners to scaffold intended learning goals to both local (institutional) and national/global (CAS) frameworks. One of the strengths of the learning and development domains is that they can be traced to other standards' learning domains, including but not limited to those found in *Learning Reconsidered* (Keeling, 2004) and the Association of American Colleges & Universities' (n.d.) Liberal Education and America's Promise, both of which are considered to be national benchmarks for learning in higher education (CAS, 2015). Similarly, as institutions determine their own learning goals and frameworks, the same comparison to the CAS domains can be made from institutional domains (L. Dean & A. Lange, webinar, January 26, 2015). For instance, MSU has five undergraduate learning goal domains, each of which can be traced back to the CAS domains. MSU's analytical thinking learning goal domain is comparable to the CAS cognitive complexity domain, while the effective citizenship learning goal is comparable to the humanitarianism and civic engagement domain (MSU Undergraduate Education, n.d.). With a grounding in both local and national frameworks, our learning outcomes and goals both achieve the missions and purposes of our institutions and programs and also meet the needs of our 21st-century learners. In other words, we have been able to be intentional about student learning in our local context while meeting a national/global need.

Absent an initiative like MSU's undergraduate learning goals, the CAS learning and development outcomes provide a framework to describe intended learning across experience and office. For instance, as colleges and universities across the United States wish to cultivate graduates who are globally engaged citizens, how can the humanitarianism and civic engagement domain be used to articulate particular dimensions of learning that all graduates should be able to experience and demonstrate when they graduate? Absent participating in a study abroad experience or engaging in globally integrated curriculum, students may never engage in learning outcomes related to the humanitarianism and civic engagement domain. Units should strive to incorporate learning goals and outcomes across CAS outcome domains.

BENCHMARKING AND INSTITUTIONAL ADVOCACY

In addition to the development of learning outcomes, the CAS standards also serve as a benchmark for good practice and a means to engage in institutional advocacy. The CAS (2009) LGBT Programs and Services standards and guidelines also call for LGBT programs and services to "promote and advocate for services addressing the unique needs of LGBT students that are generally offered by other functional areas" (p. 5). These standards and guidelines provide a framework for the base level of what LGBTQ units must advocate for, though this is not to say that advocacy can only be limited to what the standards outline.

Example in Practice: Creating a Report Focused on Good Practices

The CAS standards provide practitioners with a blueprint to conceptualize what to advocate for within the institution in order to support LGBTQ students. At MSU, we have used the CAS standards as a benchmark to formalize advocacy efforts. To that end, the MSU LBGT Resource Center developed a report focused on good practices for inclusion and equity across the institution. The *Reference Guide for Student Success and Gender Identity and Expression* (GIE) served to help administrators and practitioners meet the needs of those who are minoritized by their sex assigned at birth, gender identity, and/or gender expression. Included in the document was a section discussing which standards, according to CAS, must be present to support LGBTQ students on campus. The CAS (2009) LGBT Programs and Services standards and guidelines outlined a variety of functional areas where advocacy for LGBTQ inclusion should take place, including but not limited to counseling services, career services, public safety, library services, and student activities.

When developing the GIE, it was important to examine the other functional area standards. Due to our institutional size, we are split across multiple functional areas. CAS updates functional area standards on a rotating basis; while our services were designed using earlier iterations, the GIE was developed using the 2015 standards. For our purposes, examining the leadership, human resources, ethics, equity and access, organization and management, and internal and external relations sections in each set of functional area standards was key to understanding how those areas should address LGBTQ students' particular needs and concerns. For instance, in the Housing and Residential Life Programs standards, there is a specific call for "relationships with a wide range of student groups" (CAS, 2015, p. 298), including LGBTQ groups.

In addition to examining other functional area standards, it was important to pull in other sources of information for benchmarking to address areas not covered by the CAS standards. For instance, the Consortium's Trans* Policy Working Group developed the *Suggested Best Practices for Supporting Trans* Students* guide (Consortium of Higher Education LGBT Resource Professionals, 2014). At the time, with the LGBT Programs and Services standards and guidelines last being updated in 2009, it was important for us to collect up-to-date practice recommendations, as trans equity on college campuses has become more prominent in mainstream administrative concerns (Marine, 2011). Still, using the CAS standards as a guide for this project was important, as these standards are well-respected, vetted sources for benchmarking across higher education and student affairs.

Takeaways for Benchmarking and Institutional Advocacy

In using the CAS standards to conduct benchmarking as well as to serve as an advocacy guide, two main takeaways emerge: (1) using the CAS standards' reputation as a means of grounding advocacy efforts; and (2) using the CAS standards in conjunction with other sources of information. First, the CAS standards are vetted and agreed upon by the CAS Board of Directors and CAS member associations (CAS, 2015). In this way, the standards are assessed by a panel of those with expertise and experience in a variety of functions and functional areas in student affairs (L. Dean & A. Lange, webinar, January 26, 2015). Because of this method of creation and ongoing evaluation of the standards, the CAS standards are well-respected tools to leverage informed practice.

When practitioners and administrators begin to ask questions about why there should be certain programs or practices in place for LGBTQ students, we have been able to point to the CAS standards as a national benchmark for what we must provide and do for students. Essentially, the CAS standards continue to provide a meaningful grounding and rationale for our ongoing work.

The second major takeaway of using the CAS standards in this way is that the standards can serve as a way to root initiatives. Because of how they are developed and assessed, the CAS standards provide a foundation for program creation, design, and rationale. However, the CAS standards are updated only so often. Thus, it is important to incorporate other sources of information and rationale from emerging research and particular national organizations, like the Consortium. While we awaited updates to the CAS LGBT Programs and Services standards and guidelines, it was crucial for us to use emerging data and benchmarks to stay relevant to the needs of our students.

SELF-ASSESSMENT GUIDES

Throughout the year, many college and university offices and units collect assessment data on a variety of programs and services. These data are then used to inform future practice and learning interventions for students. However, this assessment and evaluation process generally focuses on particular programs, not on the foundation of the office or unit itself. The third way functional areas at large research institutions should use the CAS standards is through the CAS Self-Assessment Guides (SAGs). Think of the SAGs as the translations of the functional area standards and guidelines, helping practitioners gain a more informed perspective of their current level of program offerings as well as places for improvement. Rather than developing one's own tool for assessing an office or unit, the SAG format exists for practitioners to utilize and create plans of action once initial review has been completed. For more information about the SAGs, readers are encouraged to review Chapter 1 of this volume.

Example in Practice: The Process as Guided by a Summer Graduate Assistant

The CAS program review process is no small undertaking; it is a time-consuming endeavor that requires compiling documentation and evidence. Completing a SAG during the school year may be challenging; thus, the summer months can offer an important time for self-reflection and to make considerations for the following school year's practice, if that has not already been done. To that end, the MSU LBGT Resource Center every 3 to 4 years hires a summer graduate intern, generally from a student affairs and higher education graduate preparation program outside the institution, to complete a variety of summer projects. One of the intern's main projects is completing a SAG on the LGBT Programs and Services standards and guidelines for our office, in collaboration with a team of professionals. This is to ensure that we structure our programs and services in alignment with current standards and that they are relevant for a new generation of students.

In our experience, we aimed to have graduate interns collect most, if not all, of the materials and documentation needed for the review process. While it is ideal to have a team come together to complete this process, we found that much of the labor could be easily coordinated through one person. The intern compiled both existing quantitative (e.g., assessment reports, program evaluations, needs assessments) and qualitative/descriptive data (e.g., mission statements, participation policies and procedures, focus group transcripts). Once the documentation had been collected, we brought together a team of institutional and external partners and stakeholders, including students, to provide an honest appraisal of the work of the center, based on all of the materials provided in addition to their own individual experiences and perspectives.

After establishing the team, we developed a common understanding on how to interpret and use the SAG for the LGBT-focused standard. For instance, the SAGs use certain criteria for evaluating programs and services like "Partly Meets" or "Meets," as illustrated in the rating scale in Table 9.1. Team members thought through these terms and scales prior to completing individual scoring, coming to a common understanding of what each meant. Once agreement was reached, team members were given the documentation and evaluated the unit according to the standards and guidelines, using the rating scale throughout their copy of the SAG.

Table 9.1. **SAG Criterion Measure Rating Scale**

DNA	IE	0	1	2	3
Does Not Apply	Insufficient Evidence/Unable to Rate	Does Not Meet	Partly Meets	Meets	Exceeds

After compiling individual reviewers' notes and resolving gaps between ratings, any average score that fell below the "meets" score indicated that strategies would be needed to change to that particular part of our work. The team then worked to convert these strategies into an action plan that addressed the discrepancies between our current work and what the standards called for us to provide. Traditionally, our plans have included: actions required in order to meet the standard; resources needed to meet the standard (both existing resources and those that will need to be collected in the future); dates for completion; and the person(s) responsible for completing the given action.

Considerations and Takeaways for Using a SAG

Completing a SAG has great benefits for offices and units and also has benefits for graduate student interns. For instance, an intern is exposed to all areas of his or her summer work setting, gaining exposure to many different facets of the unit. In addition, completing a SAG serves to stimulate discussion topics that might not otherwise be addressed throughout the summer. Leading a SAG process can help a summer graduate intern learn more about the office, while providing a different perspective of its work; practitioners who supervise such interns should capitalize on this opportunity for outside feedback and assessment to improve programs and services, especially as student affairs has traditionally been a field that prides itself on constant reflection, feedback, assessment, and change.

While there are many benefits to conducting a self-assessment of an office or unit, there are some important considerations that need to be given before embarking on such an endeavor. For instance, the ways in which the SAGs are structured require establishing a timeline for completion as well as a team to come together to review the materials. In some instances, bringing together a team of people to work on a SAG may be easy for offices or units that have established advisory boards with a balanced makeup of internal and external stakeholders. At other times, however, a SAG may be assigned to an individual to complete, such as a graduate intern or by the internal staff of the unit. Our office takes an integrative approach, where the summer intern is charged with completing the collection and organizing the documentation as the project lead while other team members work on evaluating the particular unit. Although this approach helps to consolidate the document collection process to one person, one drawback is that the team of reviewers could get a better sense of the center's programs and services if they were to look for the documentation themselves. Thus, a limitation is that those completing a SAG may not understand the complete context of the programs and services of our office beyond the information they receive.

In addition to the makeup of the reviewer(s) in terms of background and experience, it is also important to consider the frequency of using a SAG. Our office conducts the review every 4 years to help ensure that our practice is both meeting standards and staying relevant. Due to the time and energy required to finish a SAG, a complete program review should not be completed each year or even every other year. There needs to be important thought given to the gaps in time between reviews.

CONCLUSION

This chapter outlined three ways practitioners at large research institutions can use the CAS standards in their practice, while illustrating how they are used specifically at MSU. First, practitioners can use the CAS learning and development outcome domains to guide their learning outcome design and assessment, ensuring that students are getting a breadth of exposure to different learning domains. Second, practitioners can use the standards as a benchmark for programs and services and as a means to advocate for increased attention to particular services within units and across campus. Finally, practitioners can use the SAGs to reflect on their unit's work and practice while planning for the future. The frameworks offered by CAS are multifaceted and contribute to several areas of practice within higher education, including student affairs. It remains important for student affairs educators to be committed to practice that is grounded in theory, research, assessment, and standards.

REFERENCES

American College Personnel Association. (1994). *The student learning imperative: Implications for student affairs.* Alexandria, VA: Author.

Association of American Colleges and Universities. (n.d.). About LEAP. Retrieved from https://www.aacu.org/leap

Consortium of Higher Education LGBT Resource Professionals. (2014). *Suggested best practices for supporting trans* students.* New York, NY: Author.

Council for the Advancement of Standards in Higher Education. (2009). Lesbian, gay, bisexual, transgender programs and services: CAS standards and guidelines. In L. A. Dean (Ed.), *CAS professional standards for higher education* (7th ed.). Washington, DC: Author.

Council for the Advancement of Standards in Higher Education. (2015). *CAS professional standards for higher education* (9th ed.). Washington, DC: Author.

Harper, S. R. (2011). Strategy and intentionality in practice. In J. H. Schuh, S. R. Jones, & S. R. Harper (Eds.), *Student services: A handbook for the profession* (5th ed., pp. 287–302). San Francisco, CA: Jossey-Bass.

Keeling, R. (Ed.). (2004). *Learning reconsidered: A campus-wide focus on the student experience.* Washington, DC: American College Personnel Association and National Association of Student Personnel Administrators.

Keeling, R. (Ed.). (2006). *Learning reconsidered 2: A practical guide to implementing a campus-wide focus on the student experience.* Washington, DC: American College Personnel Association, Association of College and University Housing Officers–International, Association of College Unions International, National Academic Advising Association, National Association for Campus Activities, National Association of Student Personnel Administrators, & National Intramural-Recreational Sports Association.

Komives, S. R., & Smedick, W. (2012). Using standards to develop student learning outcomes. In K. L. Guthrie & L. Osteen (Eds.), *Developing students' leadership capacity* (New Directions for Student Services, No. 140, pp. 77–88). San Francisco, CA: Jossey-Bass.

Lange, A. C. (2015). *Queer and trans community leadership outcomes 2015-2016.* East Lansing, MI: Michigan State University, Lesbian, Bisexual, Gay, and Transgender Resource Center.

Marine, S. B. (2011). *Stonewall's legacy: Bisexual, gay, lesbian, and transgender students in higher education* (ASHE Higher Education Report, Vol. 37, No. 4). San Francisco, CA: Jossey-Bass.

MSU Undergraduate Education. (n.d.). *Undergraduate learning goals at Michigan State University.* Retrieved from http://learninggoals.undergrad.msu.edu

Sanlo, R. L. (2000). The LGBT campus resource center director: The new profession in student affairs. *NASPA Journal, 37,* 485–495.

Chapter 10

Adapting the CAS Framework
The Case for Cross-Functional Standards

Léna Kavaliauskas Crain

Although the Council for the Advancement of Standards in Higher Education (CAS) publishes standards that are specific to functional areas, the CAS tools and approach can also be applied to programs and services for which specific standards do not exist. This chapter discusses a self-study conducted by the senior-year program at a large public research university.

Senior-year programs, intended for students completing their final quartile of course credits, encompass efforts related to academic, cocurricular, ritual, and career development (Henscheid, 2008). Because senior-year programs constitute an interdisciplinary area without a specific functional area set of CAS standards, student affairs staff at the University of Maryland, College Park (UMCP), creatively approached our self-assessment by applying the CAS General Standards along with excerpts from appropriately related standards (including career services, transfer student programs and services, and orientation programs, discussed later in this chapter). After completing the self-assessment, we found opportunities for future enhancement of our senior-year programs. Our successes and challenges of supporting an area without its own direct CAS tools demonstrates the adaptability of the CAS framework and makes a case for the future development of cross-functional or multifunctional CAS standards.

I approached the self-study and this chapter having professional familiarity with student transition programs, assessment, and the CAS standards and products. At the time this self-study was conducted, I had been working with students in transition for 6 years, including 3 years with first-year programs and 3 years as the senior experience coordinator at UMCP, where the study was conducted. I have served on UMCP's Student Affairs Assessment and Learning Outcomes Group for several years. As a practitioner and graduate student, I had previously used the CAS standards and Self-Assessment Guides to steer the development of new programs. In addition to my professional familiarity with the CAS standards and application to student services assessment, I served for nearly 3 years as the CAS doctoral intern, a role that exposed me to the standards development and update processes, among many other things.

CAMPUS AND DEPARTMENTAL CONTEXT

UMCP is a large, public, 4-year, research-intensive flagship institution located between Washington, D.C., and Baltimore, Maryland. UMCP is recognized as a "Public Ivy" with a highly diverse student population. UMCP's Division of Student Affairs has long been recognized for its innovation and contributions to student learning and success. In the 1990s, national demand for institutional accountability for students' postgraduate success resulted in the first senior-year programs (Gardner & Van der Veer, 1999). As a response to this demand, UMCP was among the first universities to create a senior-year program, when then vice president for student affairs Bud Thomas developed the unit (Thomas, 1999).

More than 20 years after its creation, UMCP's senior-year program continues to serve students with a mission to inform, involve, and unify senior students (University of Maryland Senior Council, 2016). A recent study of senior-year programs suggests that 97% of institutions offer them (Padgett & Kilgo, 2012). Most senior-year programs are administered in one of five ways: senior seminars and capstone courses, career preparation programs, academic synthesis showcases, celebrations and rituals, and alumni cohesion events (Henscheid, 2008). Unlike many senior-year programs, UMCP's program combines career, ritual, alumni, and educational events. UMCP's senior-year program is also unique in its organization; though many institutions house senior-year programs in career centers, academic affairs, or alumni relations offices, our program is housed in and administered from the Office of the Vice President of Student Affairs.

Senior-year programs at UMCP are administered by one half-time (20 hours per week) graduate assistant (sometimes a master's student, sometimes a doctoral student), who is referred to as the senior experience coordinator. The coordinator reports to the director of parent and family affairs, a unit that is also housed in the Office of the Vice President for Student Affairs. The senior experience coordinator advises Senior Council, a selective leadership organization of approximately 12 senior students who help to plan and execute programming. Because most senior students graduate at the conclusion of the academic year, the entirety of Senior Council members typically turns over each year. This means that the senior experience coordinator is usually the sole source of continuity and historic perspective each year. Together, the senior experience coordinator and Senior Council facilitate the senior information clearinghouse—a central gathering and dissemination source for pertinent data, deadlines, and documents—and design and execute social, educational, and philanthropic programs for senior students.

Major social events include commencement-related milestones, a senior formal dance, and senior week celebrations. Educational events include workshops related to professional success, life skills, and the post-graduation transition. Philanthropic efforts include fundraising and "friendraising" for the class gift, annual fund, and alumni association.

The UMCP senior-year experience provides a variety of programs and services with a limited budget. Annual funding for senior-year programs comes primarily from the Office of the Vice President for Student Affairs, which allocates approximately $15,000 each year for the senior experience. This amount is supplemented with grant funding, including through the Pepsi Foundation and the Maryland Parent Association, and through cosponsorship from campus departments and community organizations. External funding and sponsorships has allowed us to expand senior-year offerings despite limited fixed resources.

APPROACHING SELF-STUDY

The departmental and divisionwide climate provided an excellent opportunity for self-study. During the 2 years prior to our evaluation, senior-year programs had undergone significant changes. When I entered the role of senior experience coordinator, I worked with Senior Council members to make several changes to the programs and services at UMCP. Over time, senior-year programs had shifted primarily to social programming, and we saw an opportunity to include additional programming that reflected senior-year programs' philanthropic and educational missions. We also sought to address national conversations and trends related to employability and post-graduation success by providing active and passive programming related to tangible life skills (e.g., financial literacy) and socialization for the transition out of university (e.g., networking and apartment searching outside of college towns). We developed specific intended learning outcomes for our educational workshops and assessed students' growth based on these outcomes. For the first time in several years, senior-year programs at UMCP were addressing students' learning in strategic, thoughtful ways. This created a department-level climate of meaningful work and the opportunity to collect and measure evidence. We wanted to determine how our unit was meeting good practices, and we wanted to guide the use of resources and future decision making related to senior-year programs, so we moved toward self-study.

In addition to the changes within senior-year programs, there was also a change in the divisionwide emphasis of assessment and learning outcomes. Accreditation processes were increasingly relying on data from student services as an indicator of students' learning and development. Noting these national trends and the remarkable assessment efforts of our peer institutions, UMCP made strides to build an assessment cycle into each department in the Division of Student Affairs. The division's efforts were guided by its central Student Affairs Assessment and Learning Outcomes Group (SAALOG), which comprises representatives from each department in the Division of Student Affairs. Each department varies in size, structure, and assessment resources; some departments have dedicated assessment personnel, whereas my department had few staff members and no dedicated assessment contact. As a result, we knew our assessment efforts had to be strategically selected and were possibly limited by our resource constraints. We needed to rise to the division's expectation for assessment while working within our departmental context.

After reaching the decision to conduct a full self-assessment, we decided on a framework and tools to execute the program review. We chose the CAS standards because of my familiarity with them and because of their flexibility and utility, and we used standards from several functional areas. The CAS standards are meant to transcend context; that is, they can be applied regardless of institutional size or type, amount of resources, or organizational structure of a unit. Because of the unique position of UMCP's senior-year programs, as well as its limited and unconventional resources and staff structure, we knew the CAS standards would meet our needs for a flexible assessment framework.

DESIGNING A SELF-ASSESSMENT

To plan our self-assessment, we considered assessment tools, a project timeline, and the product that would come from our self-study. After the initial step of determining that the CAS standards would serve as our assessment framework, we realized we had to creatively combine parts of various functional area standards to create a tool for senior-year programs. Similarly, we needed data-collection tools. After speaking with others in the field, the perceived difficulty of applying the CAS standards seemed to be a common concern among practitioner–scholars who were considering using the standards in their work. The Self-Assessment Guides (SAGs) are perhaps the simplest tool for interpreting data collection related to the CAS standards; we used the 2012 version.

First, because senior-year programs do not have a specific set of standards, we used the CAS General Standards as a starting point for our self-assessment tool. The General Standards are applicable to all functional areas in higher education, designed to be used across departments, and foundational for current and future area standards development (Carretta, 2012). However, we recognized some limitations of using only the General Standards. Using them alone would not have accounted for more specific parts of the senior-year mission and programs, including efforts to address students' postgraduation success and employability, as well as the role of senior-year programs as addressing students in transition. The standards also make it challenging to account for interdepartmental efforts. Our senior-year programs unit has historically worked closely with alumni relations, special events (commencement), the career center, and many other departments, and the language of the standards and guidelines somewhat implies insular units. Thus, we knew that for our unit—a functional area that is both interdisciplinary and without specific functional area standards—we would have to creatively address the self-study. We sought to select applicable standards and guidelines from across functional areas to address senior-year programs.

The process for developing our own set of standards and guidelines, based on pieces of other functional areas to address senior-year programs, was relatively simple. First, we drew upon other standards to address more specifically the nuances of senior-year programs. Then, we developed themes in our work and mission to identify other functional areas with parallels to parts of senior-year programs' mission. For example, senior-year programs are often categorized in the literature as being geared toward a year-specific population of students in transition (Gardner & Van der Veer, 1999), so we referenced the "Program" section of the CAS standards for Transfer Student Programs and Services to understand opportunities for programming to support students in transition. Because a portion of our programming related to job-search preparation and skills related to employability, we expected to find some parallel content within career centers' materials, so we searched within the "Program" section of the CAS standards for Career Services to find guidelines suitable for career-related senior-year programs. Finally, because senior-year programs include and are guided by a student leadership organization, Senior Council, we also referenced the "Program" section of the CAS standards for Student Leadership Programs. We copied portions of the General Standards and several functional area standards, and then created a SAG to match the standards and guidelines we had selected.

After developing our tools, we determined our project timeline. We were realistic about our limitations from the outset; as most of our limitations related to staff, resources, and time, we were highly aware of the added weight of an assessment cycle to an already bare-bones organizational structure. Fortunately, the cyclical nature of the academic year and our type of work (as most seniors graduate and are replaced by a new class annually) meant that we had a natural opportunity to process data during the summer. As a result, we chose to perform the majority of the self-study during the summer months, using data collected over the course of an academic year. Our goals for the project were to shift senior-year programs at UMCP toward an evidence-based culture and to evaluate the direction of our unit, which had dramatically changed in the preceding years. The product of our study was a report used for unit reporting and for future decision making; it also provided a foundation for subsequent assessment of senior-year programs.

OPPORTUNITIES FROM CHALLENGES

Our project included several challenges, including a limited assessment culture, resource limitations, timing of the project, and nuances of the self-study process. The first challenge was a lack of assessment culture in the unit prior to our efforts. To our knowledge, no other formal, thorough program assessment had been conducted in the program's two decades. As a result, there were no formal data points, documents, or ways to evaluate growth from a previous evaluation, and we collected all evidence for the purpose of self-assessment. The limited staff structure of our unit presented a challenge and a unique opportunity for student leaders, who were able to understand more deeply their program and context as well as experience data collection and evaluation. By heavily involving students in the process, we helped them understand the importance of assessment and to recognize the significance of data in decision making that directly affected their lives.

As already mentioned, we faced significant limitations related to staff structure; this most affected the timing of our project. Conducting the self-assessment over the course of an entire academic year, especially for a first-time assessment, might have yielded more thorough evidence and a deeper understanding of all parts of the unit; however, our limited resources necessitated a shorter timeline. Next, we approached this project with an adaptable lens, out of necessity, based on our interdisciplinary unit and resource limitations. Our openness to approaching the project allowed for flexibility. For example, we had the ability to bring together portions of the standards from very different functional area standards, but that also made it harder to keep momentum and direction.

Finally, nuances of the CAS standards and self-study provided some challenges. When evaluating specific standards, we experienced some frustrations about the vagueness of some wording. For example, who can say whether our facilities are "adequate"? Based on this language, using the (2012 version) SAGs provided little clarity about how to interpret or score our progress. Despite our challenges with the task of interpreting ambiguous language, the CAS standards provided an excellent inventory through which to organize evidence, recognize strengths and deficiencies, and request changes and resources for senior-year programs.

REPORTING

After completing the self-study, we developed a report of findings that were used for external reporting and internal decision making.

We produced a narrative report and digital file of evidence. Parts of the report were used for our annual report of senior-year programs and our divisionwide notes on assessment and learning outcomes, though the majority of the report was used as an internal document to guide program development. Parts of the report were shared with the director of parent and family affairs, our unit's supervisor, as well as the assistant vice president and vice president for student affairs through the departmental annual reporting system. Finally, we shared information with the SAALOG during the annual information collection about departmental assessment projects.

Following the project, applying the findings of our self-study has made positive short- and long-term changes for senior-year programs. Because this effort was a first-time program evaluation to shift toward a culture of assessment in our unit and department, the success of our self-study was a welcome step. The project provided objective evidence to support short- and long-term changes.

In the short term, conducting a self-study helped us to become organized. We were pushed to find or create documents and processes to support our alignment with CAS standards and guidelines. The process also helped shift assessment into a more important part of our departmental culture. We made immediate and lasting decisions based on evidence collected during our self-study project.

The review also has potential long-term implications. The strengths we identified during self-study provide validation for programmatic changes made in the years prior to our project. The deficiencies we identified during the review make a case for enhanced resources for senior-year programs, especially related to staff. Based on our self-study, we hope to make a case for hiring a full-time staff member to support senior-year programs. Additionally, evaluating our programs based on multiple functional areas' standards helped us to further realize the deep connections between senior-year programs and the standards of Career Services. This knowledge supports the potential future reorganization of senior-year programs into the career services department, given the alignment of our missions. Self-study helped us to make immediate data-driven decisions as well as a case for larger, longer-term changes, all rooted in evidence.

RECOMMENDATIONS FOR PRACTICE

Our experience conducting a self-study of a functional area not directly addressed by the CAS standards demonstrates that the standards transcend institutional and departmental context to provide flexible tools that can be molded to practitioners' needs. The CAS standards and tools are designed to be flexible; they can be applied to 2- and 4-year, public and private, research-intensive or liberal arts institutions of all sizes and types. Certainly, many of the challenges we faced as a unit—especially having limited resources, staff, and time—apply to many different types of departments and campuses. In demonstrating the wide utility of the CAS standards, we have also made a case for the use of CAS on any campus and in any unit, including those departments without specific functional area standards.

The General Standards served as a solid base on which we evaluated the infrastructure of our programs. In order to address some of the specific parts of senior-year programs, we constructed an interdisciplinary set of standards. The set of standards we used were selected through careful consideration of parts of functional area standards that aligned with pieces of our mission. For example, we primarily used portions of other functional standards that addressed students' employability and the postgraduation transition. Similar opportunities exist for other units with interdisciplinary programs and services. For example, though functional area standards do not presently exist for behavioral consultation teams, teams planning a self-study might consult the standards and guidelines—especially those in the "Program" section—for Counseling Services, Sexual Violence-Related Programs and Services, and Student Conduct Programs. The CAS framework is highly flexible and adaptable to various departments, even interdisciplinary units.

CONCLUSION

In summary, using the CAS standards to evaluate an area not explicitly addressed by the standards yielded rich information for our program and for future study. We approached the self-study project with three goals: to justify changes in our unit toward good practice, to experiment with the adaptability of CAS standards and tools, and to plant the seeds for a departmental culture of data-driven decision making. Performing a self-study provided a step toward building a culture of assessment in senior-year programs at UMCP. Building upon the evidence we collected, future personnel can use our findings to justify decision making and to structure future evaluation. Conducting a self-study confirmed that our mission, programs related to employment and postgraduation success, and commitment to ethics, diversity, equity, and access were strengths. Self-study also helped us to identify opportunities for change related to enhanced staff structure, funding, and facilities. Applying different functional area standards to senior-year programs helped us to conceptualize opportunities to situate senior-year programs within other Division of Student Affairs departments, including the career center or student union. Finally, our experiment with the CAS standards confirmed the adaptability and utility of the framework, even for a program without specific functional area standards.

Practitioners seeking to evaluate their programs and services can use our process as an example of a successful self-study using a "do-it-ourselves" version of standards and guidelines created from existing CAS resources. The practice of excerpting and combining elements from different standards and guidelines showed the utility of developing cross-functional or multifunctional standards in the future, to meet the assessment needs of interdisciplinary programs such as senior-year programs.

REFERENCES

Carretta, P. (2012). CAS general standards contextual statement. In Council for the Advancement of Standards in Higher Education (Ed.), *CAS professional standards for higher education* (9th ed.). Washington, DC: Council for the Advancement of Standards in Higher Education.

Council for the Advancement of Standards in Higher Education. (2012). *CAS professional standards for higher education* (8th ed.). Washington, DC: Author.

Gardner, J. N., & Van der Veer, G. (1999). The emerging movement to strengthen the senior experience. In J. N. Gardner & G. Van der Veer (Eds.), *The senior year experience: Facilitating integration, reflection, closure, and transition*. San Francisco, CA: Jossey-Bass.

Henscheid, J. M. (2008, Winter). Institutional efforts to move seniors through and beyond college. In B. O. Barefoot (Ed.), *The first year and beyond: Rethinking the challenge of collegiate transition* (New Directions for Higher Education, No. 144, 79–87). San Francisco, CA: Jossey-Bass.

Padgett, R. D., & Kilgo, C. A. (2012). 2011 national survey of senior capstone experiences: Institutional-level data on the culminating experience. (Research Reports on College Transitions No. 3). Columbia, SC: University of South Carolina, National Resource Center for the First-Year Experience and Students in Transition.

Thomas, W. L. (1999). Mobilizing campus support for senior year programs. In J. N. Gardner & G. Van der Veer (Eds.), *The senior year experience: Facilitating integration, reflection, closure, and transition*. San Francisco, CA: Jossey-Bass.

University of Maryland Senior Council. (2016). Mission and vision. Retrieved from http://seniors.umd.edu

Chapter 11

The CAS Approach
Diverse Examples, Multiple Lessons

Needham Yancey Gulley

The Council for the Advancement of Standards in Higher Education (CAS) revolutionized how many in higher education thought about and practiced the development, implementation, and assessment of many aspects of the academy, including programs, services, and interventions. As with any revolution, what is begun by the initial founders takes on a life of its own over time—and CAS is no different. Since the CAS standards and other materials were first developed, many changes have occurred in higher education; CAS has not just kept up but has often led the way. Today, CAS continues to offer assistance to the higher education community, and, in turn, that community finds new and innovative ways to utilize CAS materials. This text includes many examples of the ways in which higher education professionals understand, engage with, and operationalize all that CAS offers.

This book frames how the CAS standards might be useful to higher education professionals in a variety of settings and contexts. Readers should think critically and creatively about taking advantage of all that CAS has to offer and how to use the CAS standards as a springboard for going beyond what the standards address directly; for example, Chapter 10 described how CAS can inform practice in functional areas for which standards have not been developed. The CAS standards offer guidelines for practice, yet they are flexible enough to respond to nuances of institutional structure, diversity of functional area design, and other unique contexts. In synthesizing what has been presented, this conclusion highlights similarities across chapters, unique perspectives, and a few additional considerations that have been brought to light in response to the work of the authors.

SIMILARITIES ACROSS CHAPTERS

Looking back across the chapters in this text, it is clear that many of the contributing authors use the CAS standards to inform assessments of programs and services. They discussed the ways in which they conceptualized the review process and how they intentionally created systems and procedures to guide these assessments. While there are different examples for how this is accomplished, there are also some consistent points that emerge. For instance, many of the contributors discussed the importance of gaining buy-in from the campus community and of offering intensive training to those who are part of the assessment process. There are a variety of strategies to create the buy-in necessary to successfully implement the CAS standards. In order to gauge which method might be best for your environment, it is helpful to assess the readiness for CAS among the necessary stakeholders. If you already have support for assessment- and outcomes-driven practice, you may not need to work as hard to gain buy-in, and you may be able to move more quickly into the assessment work. However, if your team (department, division, institution) is not as inclined or is reticent to engage in evaluation, you will need to determine how to assuage fears and facilitate an understanding of the benefits of such practice. Several ways to gain such buy-in are outlined throughout the chapters. Some ways include having a senior campus leader champion the cause; contextualizing the use of the CAS standards in relation to existing demands for accountability, such as reaffirmation of accreditation; sharing the positive outcomes associated with the use of the CAS standards from an aspirant institution; and connecting the use of the CAS standards to fulfilling the demands of the completion agenda. Often a grassroots effort, gaining buy-in is about building one-on-one relationships across the institution.

When you have determined that there is sufficient buy-in to move forward with using the CAS standards within your institutional context (department or division), it is time to train those who will take part. In thinking about who will constitute the team, it is important to be strategic and intentional. It is best to bring in a people with a variety of backgrounds—and those that can work well together. As some of the contributing authors noted, training is integral to successful implementation. Training should start with the philosophical underpinnings of the CAS standards and locating the standards within the larger context of higher education. Next, training on the General Standards and functional area standards, and the variety of uses that exist for these standards, will help stakeholders see how using the CAS standards could assist in a variety of ways. Once some of these big-picture ideas have been presented and understood, attention can be paid to specific uses of the CAS standards and the particular components to be used. By scaffolding training in this way, participants can easily understand how everything fits together and connects back to the larger purpose of overall assessment.

Chapter authors also consistently discussed the importance of designating leaders for the assessment process. Some suggested that, in their contexts, it was helpful to have an individual staff person dedicated to the assessment process; others noted that developing a team to manage the review process was most beneficial. Contributors also used the CAS standards in a variety of ways, from assessing existing programming to developing new programs and services. These different functions, along with consideration of institutional culture, should drive how leadership for assessment is decided and utilization of the CAS standards is designed.

UNIQUE PERSPECTIVES ACROSS CHAPTERS

It is important to acknowledge here the diverse and unique voices that fill this text. Contributors were intentionally selected for their varied experiences in engaging with the CAS standards. This range of voices highlights the myriad ways that the CAS standards can be used in as many institutional types as possible. Readers may have noticed points where authors are in agreement and where certain concepts or approaches are reiterated across chapters—as well as places where contributors offer examples, understandings, or recommendations that contradict one another. This is one of the strengths of the CAS standards: their flexibility. As you have read, along with the CAS standards there are many supports to help scaffold their implementation, such as the learning and development outcomes and Self-Assessment Guides. However, the standards continue to be applied in a variety of creative ways that make specific sense for the particular context in which they are being used. Chapter 3 outlined how the General Standards can be helpful for program development and assesment; other chapters noted focusing initially on relevant parts of specific standards to lay the foundation for a later full program review. The CAS standards are a terrific guide that can be interpreted and tweaked in order to make sense for your setting.

Another concept that several contributing authors discussed is the notion of a cycle of assessment. In the higher education context, a cycle of assessment is the process of evaluating outcomes and using the results to improve practice; these chapters reflect the additional idea of developing a schedule of when and how programs and services will be evaluated, again with the goal of using the findings for overall improvement. This idea is strongly linked to the concept of continuous improvement. Continuous improvement is the loop of identifying a need for an intervention or service, defining necessary outcomes, designing a program to address those outcomes, implementing the program or service, assessing learning and effectiveness, making adjustments based on data, and repeating the process.

It is also important to recognize that terms like *cycle of assessment* and *continuous improvement* are similarly defined and often used interchangeably. Applying these concepts in tandem helps to keep assessment on track and allows for the maximization of resources, especially those related to time and staff allocation. Defining your cycle of assessment is particularly crucial in institutions where there are multiple departments conducting assessments on a regular basis. In those cases, it is important to work across the institution to coordinate an overall schedule that allows for all assessments to be conducted without overtaxing resources at any one time.

ADDITIONAL CONSIDERATIONS FOR USING CAS

Beyond some of the areas discussed above—that were addressed in several chapters—two additional good practices when using the CAS standards should be highlighted. The first has to do with transparency and is closely tied to obtaining and keeping buy-in from stakeholders. It is important to be clear about what the process of using the CAS standards looks like at your institution. For example, if you are using the CAS standards as a guide for program review, then you should share what the steps for that review are, how data are collected and evaluated, and how the results will be used, so that others can follow the process and trust the results. This is particularly important because sometimes the findings of a review show that substantial change is necessary. Willingness to be transparent about the process can help to alleviate concerns about trust. Similarly, the second recommended good practice is showing how results of program reviews and assessments are used to make adjustments as part of a continuous improvement plan. In higher education, as in many settings, faculty, staff, and students often feel that evaluative data are collected and reviewed but not utilized. That perception can make it difficult to trust the process or see the value of engaging in it. To combat this skepticism, it is crucial to show that assessment findings and recommendations are leading to change.

If you are thinking of using the CAS standards at your institution, here are some questions you might consider:

- Which key stakeholders will support the utilization of the CAS standards and process?
- Which key stakeholders will potentially be resistant to implementing the CAS program review process? Who and/or what might convince them that using the CAS standards will be beneficial to practice?
- What is the familiarity with assessment as a whole, and with the CAS standards specifically, at your institution, within your division, and among individual departments and practitioners?
- How much training is necessary to prepare for a CAS program review process, and how might that training be accomplished? Do you have the expertise within, or do you have the resources to bring someone in to assist you?
- What are the most useful resources developed by CAS for your department, division, or institution?

- In what ways might the CAS standards be helpful (e.g., developing a new program, designing learning outcomes, benchmarking, training staff, conducting program review, etc.)?

When answering these questions and others like them, consider available resources across the entire institution, as support for your efforts might be found outside of one department or even one division. Further, consider if you can advocate for implementation or adoption of the CAS standards and/or if there is benefit to bringing in outside experts to validate utilization. There are times that these things can be accomplished internally, but in some cases it might be best to have some outside assistance. Keep the end goals in mind and look internally to understand your local culture enough to assess the best way forward.

FINAL THOUGHTS

It is important to remember that regardless of your institutional type or functional area, the CAS standards can be incredibly valuable in developing and assessing a variety of programs, services, and outcomes. This text brings together diverse voices from multiple perspectives in order to provide insight into the on-the-ground use of the standards and the lessons to be learned. As you engage with the standards, be creative, be thoughtful, and be focused on how you can improve your practice.

Appendix A

CAS Self-Study
Roles, Responsibilities, and Timeline

Role of the Self-Study Coordinator

- Recommend appropriate individuals to serve on the review team.
- Identify any Council for the Advancement of Standards in Higher Education (CAS) guidelines that are to be used as standards and write criterion statements for them to be included in the Self-Assessment Guide (SAG); make any further recommendations for editorial changes to the SAG.
- Submit a list of documentary evidence, indexed across the 12 component areas, and a proposed timeline to the assistant vice president for student affairs for feedback.
- Collect departmental-level documentary evidence and prepare a Canvas Course or DropBox folder, indexed across the 12 component areas, to be shared with each team member.
- After the initial team orientation, plan and facilitate all subsequent meetings and correspondence with the team members.
- Collect the individual ratings from the team members and submit them for compilation to the assistant vice president for student affairs.

- Serve as the primary author of the executive summary and action plan, seeking interpretation on findings, input on decisions, and editing on final document from the review team.
- Complete tasks in accordance with the agreed upon deadlines.

Role of the Assistant Vice President for Student Affairs

- Formally invite participants identified by the self-study coordinator to serve on the review team and coordinate the scheduling of the opening orientation meeting.
- Collect *relevant* materials and results from previous CAS self-studies and campuswide standardized surveys (National Survey of Student Engagement, Student Satisfaction Inventory, Cooperative Institutional Research Program [CIRP] Freshman Survey, etc.).
- Prepare and distribute edited version of the appropriate SAG.
- Provide documentary evidence for the component areas heavily influenced at the institutional level, including Part 4–Human Resources; Part 6–Law, Policy, and Governance; Part 9–Financial Resources; Part 10–Technology; and Part 11–Facilities and Assessment.
- Approve tentative list of department-level documentary evidence materials and a timeline for the self-study.
- Schedule and facilitate the opening orientation meeting of the review team, where the purpose, roles, expectations, timeline, and printed copy of the SAG for the CAS self-study are presented.
- Prepare a collective group rating of each criterion measure as well as a consolidated summary of all individual ratings, rationale comments, and responses to the overview questions.
- Collect and disseminate the Executive Summary and Action Plan to the appropriate stakeholders.
- Complete tasks in accordance with the agreed-upon deadlines.

Role of the CAS Review Team

- Attend a minimum of four meetings throughout the CAS self-study process.
- Complete an individual rating of each criterion statement using the scale provided in the edited SAG.
- Participate in a group interpretation of the collective ratings and help determine appropriate corrective actions and/or steps for program enhancements whenever there are discrepancies between the CAS standards and practice.
- Help edit an Executive Summary and Action Plan, drafted by the self-study coordinator.
- Complete tasks in accordance with the agreed-upon deadlines.

PROPOSED TIMELINE FOR CAS SELF-STUDY	
By early August	• Consider membership to the CAS review team. • Prepare a list of documentary evidence to be collected and indexed across the 12 component areas; begin collection process. • Prepare a timeline for the CAS self-study. • Recommend editorial revisions for the SAG. Notes:
By early September	• Have initial orientation meeting with the assistant vice president for student affairs and review team where the purpose, roles, expectations, timeline, and revised SAG for the CAS self-study are presented. • Complete the collection and index of documentary evidence to be made available to each team member via Canvas or Dropbox. Notes:

PROPOSED TIMELINE FOR CAS SELF-STUDY

By early October	• Having had time to go through the SAG once, facilitate a second meeting with the review team to discuss questions and missing information, and clarify expectations regarding the individual ratings of the SAG items. Notes:
By mid-November	• Facilitate a third meeting with the review team to collect all completed individual assessments and discuss any lingering issues. • Submit to assistant vice president for student affairs individual ratings from the team members for summary analysis and consolidation of all notes and comments. Notes:
By early February	• Have fourth meeting with review team to interpret the collective ratings and discuss appropriate corrective actions and/or steps for program enhancements whenever there are discrepancies between the standards and practice. Notes:
By mid-February	• Have fifth meeting with review team to discuss final draft of Executive Summary and Action Plan. Notes:
By mid-June	Finalize Executive Summary and Action Plan and submit to assistant vice president for student affairs to be forwarded to the vice president for student affairs. Notes:

Appendix B

CAS Review Executive Summary and Action Plan

I. **Summarize the Self-Assessment Process:** Identify the members of the self-assessment review team and describe the process and timeline for the self-study.

II. **Provide a Narrative Response to Each Overview Question:** For each of the 12 overview areas, please provide a short summary response.

Part 1: Mission Overview Questions

A. What is the program[1] mission, and when was it last revised?

B. How does the program mission support student learning, development, and success?

C. In what ways does the program mission complement the mission of the institution?

D. How is the program mission made visible, and to what extent is it used to guide practice?

---

[1] Use of the term "program" can be interpreted in multiple ways, based on context; it can include multiple program areas and services, depending on the departmental structure.

Part 2: Program Overview Questions

A. Describe the primary elements/components of the program and how they reflect the program mission.

B. What are the program's most significant student learning and development outcomes?

C. What evidence exists to confirm that the program contributes to student learning, development, and success?

Part 3: Organization and Leadership Overview Questions

A. To what extent and how are personnel responsibilities, expectations, and standards for communication clearly shared?

B. Describe evidence found of effective leadership practices within the program area.

C. Describe the present opportunities and limitations as the staff seek to fulfill the program mission.

Part 4: Human Resources Overview Questions

A. What are the pressing concerns related to staffing the program?

B. In what ways are training and professional development, supervision, and evaluation of each staff member provided?

C. To what degree does the staffing structure reflect the mission and needs of the program?

D. In what ways are student workers, interns, and/or graduate students utilized?

Part 5: Ethics Overview Questions

A. What ethical principles, standards, statements, or codes guide the program and its staff members?

B. What is the program's strategy for managing student and staff confidentiality and privacy issues?

C. Describe how any ethical dilemmas and decisions and/or conflicts of interest have been resolved.

Part 6: Law, Policy, and Governance Overview Questions

A. What are the crucial legal issues faced by the program, and how are they addressed?

B. How are staff kept abreast of changing laws, regulations, and policies where noncompliance can result in legal risks and liabilities?

Part 7: Diversity, Equity, and Access Overview Questions

A. How does the program ensure nondiscriminatory, fair, and equitable treatment to all constituents?

B. What policies and/or practices are in place to address imbalances in participation among selected categories of students and any lack of diverse perspectives among staff members?

C. How are the multicultural competencies of student and professional staff developed?

Part 8: Internal and External Relations Overview Questions

A. With which relevant individuals, groups, campus offices, and external agencies must the program maintain critical partnerships?

B. What evidence confirms effective relationships with both internal and external program constituents?

C. In what ways do the leaders engage in collaboration with campus partners?

Part 9: Financial Resources Overview Questions

A. What are the immediate concerns related to the procurement and disbursement of funds?

B. To what degree are outside sources of funding utilized?

C. What evidence exists to confirm fiscal responsibility, responsible stewardship, and cost-effectiveness?

Part 10: Technology Overview Questions

A. What are the pressing concerns related to technology?

B. Describe any recent issues or concerns related to information confidentiality and security.

C. In what ways is technology used to enhance the marketing, quality, and delivery of programs and services?

Part 11: Facilities and Equipment Overview Questions

A. What are the immediate concerns related to facilities and equipment?

B. What evidence exists to confirm facilities and equipment access as well as the health, safety, and security for all who are served by the program?

Part 12: Assessment Overview Questions

A. Describe the program's current assessment practices.

B. What evidence exists to ensure that the stated mission, program goals and objectives, and student learning and development outcomes are achieved?

C. In what ways have assessment and evaluation results been used to revise and improve the quality of programs and services?

III. **Identify Areas of Program Strength**: Given the Self-Assessment Guide (SAG) 4-point rating scale of 0 to 3, a rating of 2.0 or higher indicates that an area "Met" or "Exceeded" the standard. Of the 12 component areas, summarize each with an overall collective rating of 2.0 or higher, highlighting any chosen significant accomplishments.

IV. **Note items with ratings of "Does Not Apply" (DNA), "Insufficient Evidence/Unable to Rate" (IE), and significant discrepancy.**

   A. Summarize any items that were rated as DNA.

   B. Summarize the items that were rated as IE.

   C. Summarize the items where significant discrepancy (more than 2 points) among the raters was observed.

V. **Write an Action Plan for Areas That Need Development:** Given the SAG 4-point rating scale of 0 to 3, a rating of 1.9 or lower indicates that an area "Did Not Meet" or "Partially Met" the standard. Of the 12 component areas, identify each with an overall collective rating of 1.9 or lower. Considering importance, need, and achievability, prioritize these measures and write an action plan for each, specifying what needs to be done to address the shortcomings. (*Note*: Additional initiatives can be suggested to enhance program quality and effectiveness that do not necessarily reflect lower ratings.)

For each action plan recommendation:

   A. Identify resources (e.g., human, fiscal, physical) that are essential to program enhancement.

   B. Set dates by which specific actions are to be completed.

   C. Identify responsible parties to complete the action steps.

IV. **Appendices:** Please attach a copy of the collective ratings as an appendix to this document.

Note. Language is taken from *CAS Professional Standards for Higher Education* (9th ed.) and revised for internal use at Longwood University.

Appendix C

Reference Sheet for Completing Outcome Planning

The worksheet on the following page outlines the link between university values, student affairs mission, vision, goals, and CAS learning outcomes.

Date:	Division Goal 2016–2017: Promoting values, ethics, responsibility, and wellness.			
Department:	Objective:			
Tasks to Accomplish Objective	Current Trend Data (citations)	Collaborative Partners	Task Deadline	Measuring Outcome Data/ Collection Method
1. Target Learning Outcome:				
2. Target Learning Outcome:				
3. Target Learning Outcome:				

See next page, "University Mission: Changing Lives Through Education," for reference information.

University Mission: Changing Lives Through Education		
UNCP Values	**Student Affairs Mission Statement**	**CAS Student Learning Outcomes**
Communication: talk to each other, inform each other	The Division of Student Affairs empowers students to succeed, facilitates active learning, develops cultural appreciation, promotes responsible citizenship, and ensures a robust campus experience for student engagement.	**Knowledge, acquisition, construction, integration, and application:** understanding, connecting, constructing, and relating knowledge to daily life
Collaboration: work together for a common purpose		**Cognitive complexity:** ways of thinking—critical, reflective, effective, creative
	Student Affairs Vision Statement	
Integrity: do what is right for the right reason	The Division of Student Affairs strives to transform students into lifelong learners who contribute responsibly to society.	**Intrapersonal development:** realistic self-appraisal, identity development, commitment to ethics/integrity, spiritual awareness
	Student Affairs Goals	
Accountability: own your actions and your responsibilities	**1. Robust campus:** Create a robust campus environment. We will reimagine and create physical space to foster our campus environment.	**Interpersonal development:** meaningful relationships, interdependence, collaboration, effective leadership
Innovation: create meaning, do more with less	**2. Enriching experience:** Develop enriching student experiences. We will develop opportunities that connect students with self-defined purposes.	**Humanitarianism and civic engagement:** understanding and appreciating cultural difference, global perspective, social and civic responsibility

University Mission: Changing Lives Through Education		
UNCP Values	**Student Affairs Mission Statement**	**CAS Student Learning Outcomes**
Service: focus on others' needs ahead of your own	**3. Student wellness:** Provide a campus experience that encourages students to embrace ethical standards and values that are congruent with those of the university. We will promote the understanding of the university's core values in order to support the personal wellness of each student.	**Practical competence:** pursuing goals, communicating effectively, technological competence, managing personal affairs, managing career, demonstrating professionalism, maintaining health and wellness, living a purposeful life
We strive to keep this process easy and clear; we can only do this with feedback from all of our stakeholders. Please send any feedback about this form, the assessment process, and/or department strategic planning to the SA Assessment Committee.	**4. Support diversity:** Create an inclusive, diverse, and respectful campus. We will leverage the diversity of our community to develop a better sense of cultural appreciation and to teach and model cultural competency.	*Please consider using the mission, vision, and values of UNCP in the development of your department plans. Consider the language of our UNCP values. The CAS learning outcomes will be connected to every task designed to meet your department objective.*
	5. Sustainability: Cultivate a sustainable campus for student success. We will leverage staff, faculty, community talent, knowledge, and skills to support the professional development of our community.	

Division of Student Affairs
Directions for Planning and Assessment Worksheet

Important things to remember:

1. Please do not change the layout of the form.
2. Each worksheet contains ONE priority. Place different priorities on different tabbed worksheets.

Category	Directions
Department	List the name of your department.
Completion Date	Record your **projected** date of completion for the priority listed on that worksheet.
Name of Priority	Create a name (succinct, yet descriptive) for your annual priority, and place it here. Reference the Student Affairs or Enrollment Management Strategic Plan for specific language used in those plans; this way, your worksheet related to any strategic priority reflects that language.

Category	Directions
Departmental Goal	Identify your Departmental Goal that most closely aligns with your proposed Annual or Strategic Planning Priority. Make sure that over a 5-year period you identify Annual Priorities (or other initiatives) to address each of your Departmental Goals at least one time, preferably more. **Note:** Your program goals are broad statements that describe the overarching, long-range intended outcomes of an administrative unit. Goals are related to the mission of the department and are not necessarily measurable. You reach your goals by establishing specific planning priorities with specific outcomes (achievement or assessment targets). The program goal is the starting point for the development and refinement of outcomes. Departments reported their program goals in the Annual Report—these should remain constant over years.
Strategic Planning Goal	Check the Strategic Planning Goal that best aligns with your Departmental Goal. Reference appropriate worksheets.
Type of Priority	Select the type of priority from the list provided. FY__ planning expectations indicate that departments complete 4 total priorities, with at least 2 priorities focusing on student learning. Additional information about expectations is included in the **Expectations tab**.
Resources Needed/ Reallocated	Indicate any new resources needed or resources you will reallocate. Only select "New Staff" if you will be requesting additional staff as part of the budget process to complete this priority. This section should align with your budget requests for FY__.
Action Steps and Timeline	List the specific steps you will employ to complete your priority. After each numbered step, include the month that you anticipate completing that step of your plan. Use this checklist to help build your Action Steps and Timeline. ☐ Steps are broken down into discrete tasks and arranged in a numbered list. ☐ Steps include how collaborative partners will be involved in accomplishing the priority. ☐ Steps include references to timeline. ☐ All assessment methods listed on Planning Worksheet are clearly addressed (named) in the Action Steps. ☐ Steps are written with minimal department-specific jargon.
Method (Direct and Indirect)	Indicate how you will collect your data. Try to limit the number of methods selected to no more than 3, preferable 1–2. You MAY select both direct with indirect for each priority. A description of each method is included in Appendix C, if needed. **Note:** Selecting observation as a method will necessitate the development of a checklist or other rubric to formalize any data you obtain via observation.
Collaborative Partners	Indicate the areas/departments you will collaborate with to accomplish the priority. An "other" option is available to indicate a different collaborative partner than those listed, or to specify within a collaborative partner area (e.g., Student Affairs and Enrollment Management).

Category	Directions
Expected Student Learning Outcomes	If you selected "Learning Focused" in the "Type of Priority" box, check the learning outcome and/or related goal that aligns with your priority. This section is based on outcomes proposed by *Learning Reconsidered* (2004). Resources to assist you with this section can be found in Appendices D and E. Review the sample developmental experiences for learning listed (Appendix D) to help discern where your department's priority aligns. You may list another learning or program effectiveness outcome if those offered do not align with your priority. REMEMBER: Two of your priorities must be student learning–oriented.
Available Data	Summarize the existing data related to this priority (e.g., local, statewide, national). If no data are available, you may insert "no data available." Number/letter these and align them with the Assessment Targets (also numbered/lettered).
Assessment Targets/ Measurable Outcomes/ Objectives	These are your exact assessment target(s). List them (use numbers or letters) for the stated priority. Align these targets/outcomes/ objectives with the numbered/lettered list in Available Data, so that Available Data Item #1 or A is your baseline data for the Target #1 or A. This target is specific and measurable and is informed by earlier data (if available). **In most cases, the target(s) should be quantitative in nature.** Use this checklist to help build your targets/ outcomes/objectives. Note: These items are **not** expected to align with the numbering used in the Action Steps and Timeline section. Is the target/outcome/objective: ☐ An important/significant outcome you hope the initiative will achieve? ☐ Meaningful to achieve given departmental goals? ☐ Manageable to achieve given time and other resources available? ☐ Measurable to achieve a given type of target, staff training, experience, etc.? ☐ Related to the *Learning Reconsidered* (or other Program Effectiveness) outcome associated with the Priority? (Learning outcome selected should have an associated target/objective.)

Department Annual Summary
Student Affairs

Date:

Department:

OBJECTIVES AND TIMELINES

Objective #1: Green Sheet 1: Provide comprehensive interpersonal violence prevention outreach.

Task to Accomplish Objective	Measurement Data Collected	Assessment Target	Objective Status and Learning Outcomes
Example: Execute 3 distinct awareness campaigns; October – Bullying January – Stalking April – Sexual Assault	1. Number of days the stalking/ bullying posters are up on campus. 2. Number of students taking the "these hands are not for hurting" pledge and putting handprints on the display.	• 90% compliance with all outreach deadlines. • 90+ students taking the pledge.	All targets were met. Learning Outcome: The 105 students taking the pledge "these hands are not for hurting" clearly articulated an understanding of the importance of non-violence in relationships.

Objective #2:
Strategies and Timelines

Strategy	Measurement Data Collected	Assessment Target	Strategy Status and Learning Outcomes

Objective #3:
Strategies and Timelines

Strategy	Measurement Data Collected	Assessment Target	Strategy Status

Please write a short paragraph outlining the achievements and challenges in each area. Specifically focus on what your department will change, keep, or delete in the upcoming year.

- **Learning outcomes:** On what learning outcomes did the department focus? What learning outcomes will you continue, add or drop for next year?

- **Finance:** *(% budget used, budget short falls, % spent on specific goals—professional development, student training, etc.)*

  Do you think you spent this wisely, what can be improved, what can be better for next year...?

- **Personnel:** *(promotion, retirement, new positions, internships)*

- **Professional achievements:**

- **Programmatic review:** *(e.g., We ran eight groups, one was closed for lack of attendance. We plan to run that group again in the fall with new advertising and an improved curriculum.)*

- **Collaborative efforts:**

- **Committees:**

- **Special projects/events:**

CAS Student Learning and Development Domains and Dimensions

Domain	Dimensions
Knowledge acquisition, integration, construction, and application	Understanding knowledge from a range of disciplines; connecting knowledge to other knowledge, ideas, and experiences; constructing knowledge; and relating knowledge to daily life
Cognitive complexity	Critical thinking; reflective thinking; effective reasoning; and creativity
Intrapersonal development	Realistic self-appraisal, self-understanding, and self-respect; identity development; commitment to ethics and integrity; and spiritual awareness
Interpersonal competence	Meaningful relationships; interdependence; collaboration; and effective leadership
Humanitarianism and civic engagement	Understanding and appreciation of cultural and human differences; social responsibility; global perspective; and sense of civic responsibility
Practical competence	Pursuing goals; communicating effectively; technical competence; managing personal affairs; managing career development; demonstrating professionalism; maintaining health and wellness; and living a purposeful and satisfying life

Note. Adapted from *CAS Professional Standards for Higher Education* (p. 25), by the Council for the Advancement of Standards in Higher Education, 2015, Washington, DC: Author. Copyright © 2015 by the Council for the Advancement of Standards in Higher Education. Adapted with permission.

The Authors

Léna Kavaliauskas Crain has worked with students in transition for 6 years—3 years with first-year programs and 3 years with the senior-year experience. Her work with senior-year programs at the University of Maryland, College Park (UMCP), was recognized nationally as an Exceptional Practice by ACPA–College Student Educators International. Crain's research interests include transition, dimensions of national culture, professional socialization, and postgraduation success. She served as the Council for the Advancement of Standards in Higher Education (CAS) doctoral intern for nearly 3 years and is a staff member at UMCP, where she received her PhD.

Laura A. Dean is a professor in the College Student Affairs Administration program at the University of Georgia. Before joining the faculty, she served as the senior student affairs officer at Pfeiffer University and at Peace College in North Carolina. She earned her undergraduate degree in English from Westminster College in Pennsylvania and both of her graduate degrees, in counselor education/student development in higher education, from The University of North Carolina at Greensboro. A member of ACPA–College Student Educators International, NASPA–Student Affairs Administrators in Higher Education, the American Counseling Association, and the American College Counseling Association (ACCA), Dean was active with the Council for the Advancement of Standards in Higher Education for nearly 20 years, including service as editor of the *CAS Professional Standards for Higher Education* (6th and 7th editions) and as president. She has been recognized with the

ACPA Diamond Honoree and Senior Professional Annuit Coeptis awards, ACCA's Professional Leadership Award, and the NASPA Robert H. Shaffer Award for Academic Excellence as a Graduate Faculty Member. Her research focuses on assessment, the use of professional standards, and small college issues.

Shannon R. Dean is an assistant professor in student affairs in higher education at Texas State University. She teaches courses in student development theory, assessment, evaluation, strategic planning, research methods, and internship experiences in higher education. Dean's current research focuses on multicultural consciousness of undergraduate students, teaching pedagogies, faculty–student interactions, as well as the experiences of new professionals utilizing theory in their practice. Prior to joining the faculty, Dean's professional experience included administrative roles in various functional areas such as housing and residence life, service–learning, academic advising, leadership development and civic engagement, and international student life.

Deborah Garrett is the vice chancellor for student services at Arkansas State University–Beebe and also serves as the president of the Council for the Advancement of Standards in Higher Education. Garrett has served in higher education for almost 40 years, with roles as a senior-level student affairs professional and interim college president. She has a passion for improving programming and services for students through implementing self-assessment and incorporating student learning outcomes.

Needham Yancey Gulley spent 15 years as a college administrator (primarily at 2-year colleges) prior to moving into a faculty role. Most of his administrative career has been in the area of student affairs. He has worked at several institutions, including Louisburg College,

North Carolina State University, Long Beach City College, the University of Georgia, and Athens Technical College. He currently serves as an assistant professor of higher education and student affairs at Western Carolina University. Gulley has a long history of advocating for social justice within the educational context, through his scholarship, teaching, publications, presentations, trainings, and volunteer endeavors. He recently completed a research project focused on the nature of collaboration between academic and student affairs units in the community college setting. His past research not only contributed to the scholarly conversation in higher education and student affairs, but it also led to changes in the academy, including the opening of the Lesbian, Gay, Bisexual, and Transgender Resource Center at North Carolina State University. Currently, he is researching the experiences of lesbian, gay, bisexual, transgender, and queer community college students, as well as the experiences of White faculty working at historically Black colleges and universities.

John R. Jones III is vice president for student affairs at The University of Alabama at Birmingham (UAB). Prior to joining UAB, he served as vice chancellor for student affairs at the University of North Carolina at Pembroke, associate vice president in the Division of Student Affairs and Enrollment Management at Northern Illinois University, and assistant vice chancellor and associate dean of students in the Division of Student Life and Diversity at Indiana University–Purdue University Indianapolis. He holds a bachelor's degree in applied mathematics from Appalachian State University and both master's and doctoral degrees in higher education administration from The University of Iowa. He is an active member of NASPA–Student Affairs Administrators in Higher Education and ACPA–College Student Educators International and has served on the board of directors for the Madame Walker Urban Life Center in Indianapolis,

Indiana; the Center for Academic Integrity; and the Association for Student Conduct Administration.

Alex C. Lange currently serves as the assistant director of the Lesbian, Bisexual, Gay, and Transgender Resource Center at Michigan State University. Lange's research interests, praxis, and publications have centered on transgender/gender nonconforming student engagement, socially responsible leadership, and queer student leadership and activism. Lange has been honored as an Annuit Coeptis Emerging Professional by ACPA–College Student Educators International. Lange holds a master's degree in college student affairs administration from the University of Georgia and a bachelor's degree in law and American society from the Wilkes Honors College at Florida Atlantic University.

David Mayes is associate vice chancellor for student services/dean of students at Arkansas State University–Beebe. He has more than 20 years of experience in student services, with such responsibilities as student conduct administration, student housing, student government, student activities, student organizations, student leadership programs, enrollment management, and Title IX compliance.

Onie McKenzie oversees outcomes assessment, strategic planning, and professional development as the assistant vice president for student affairs at Longwood University, having previously directed academic assessment both at Longwood University and Hampden-Sydney College. Additionally, she directly supports the work of the Student Engagement Unit, overseeing Citizen Leadership and Social Justice Education, University Operations and Student Activities, and Fraternity and Sorority Life. She received her bachelor's degree from the University of the South in Sewanee, Tennessee, and also completed advanced graduate studies at the University of Georgia and the University of Virginia. Her work in student affairs began in career services at Whitman College in Washington, and she has served in a number of different professional association volunteer positions and on two commission directorate boards for ACPA–College Student Educators International.

Tim James Pierson is vice president for student affairs at Longwood University. He began his tenure at Longwood in 1992 as the dean of students, serving in that role until 2000, when he was promoted to his current position. He previously served as the dean of residence life at Willamette University in Salem, Oregon; director of student affairs for Lyman Briggs College, Michigan State University (MSU); and head resident advisor at MSU. He holds bachelor's and master's degrees from Central Michigan University and a doctorate in higher education administration from MSU. He is an active member of both ACPA–College Student Educators International and NASPA–Student Affairs Administrators in Higher Education and is the recipient of the 2005 ACPA Excellence in Practice Award.

Mary-Jeanne Raleigh began her higher education career in housing and residence life, moving to the position of director of clinical health services and working her way up to the position of director of counseling and psychological services at the University of North Carolina at Pembroke (UNCP). These career movements allowed her to develop a comprehensive understanding of the interconnected work of student affairs departments and the critical elements of assessment for learning outcomes. She is an active member of the American College Counseling Association (ACCA), the American Counseling Association, the Association of University and College Counseling Center Directors, and the Association of Counseling Educators and Supervisors. For more than 8 years, she has represented ACCA on the Council for the Advancement of Standards in Higher Education

(CAS) Board of Directors. Most recently, she completed a review and updating of the CAS Clinical Health Services standards and designed and executed UNCP's Division of Student Affairs CAS assessment protocols.

Adrian Rodriguez is vice president for student development services at Tarrant County College, River Campus, in Fort Worth, Texas. He has served in this role for 7 years and appreciates that no day is the same; each always brings a new way to impact students' lives. Rodriguez has previously served in a variety of roles, including dean of students, registrar, director of student activities, director of residence life, director of intramurals, and—one of his personal favorites— college fastpitch softball coach. He earned his Bachelor of Science degree in environmental design at Texas A&M University and his Master of Science degree in educational administration from Texas A&M University–Kingsville. Rodriguez is a doctoral student in the Student Affairs in Higher Education, Counseling, and Educational Psychology program at Kansas State University.

Dave Rozeboom is vice president for student life at Hardin-Simmons University (HSU). For 19 years he has held administrative positions in higher education, including director of residence life at St. Edward's University and assistant director for campus living and learning at Baylor University. These roles have afforded him opportunities to serve in a wide variety of ways, including leading assessment and retention efforts. He also has a strong teaching back-ground, having taught high school mathematics classes, undergrad-uate-level leadership courses at Baylor University, a senior capstone class and graduate-level counseling and student development courses at St. Edward's University, and doctoral leadership classes at HSU. He holds a BA in mathematics/secondary education from Calvin

College in Grand Rapids, Michigan; an MA in higher education administration from the University of Akron in Ohio; and a PhD in educational administration and a college teaching certification from Texas A&M University.

Louann Schulze is director of counseling at Tarrant County College–Trinity River Campus in Fort Worth, Texas. In this role, she supervises advising and counseling, disability support services, testing, career services, the New Student Welcome Center, and the Transfer Center. Her career in higher education includes both 4-year universities and community colleges in the areas of counseling, advising, new student orientation, and student services administration. She is a licensed professional counselor in Texas. She holds a BA in psychology from Texas State University, an MS in counseling from Texas A&M University, and an EdD in higher education administration from the University of North Texas.

Marybeth Drechsler Sharp is executive director of the Council for the Advancement of Standards in Higher Education. She completed her doctorate in college student personnel at the University of Maryland, College Park (UMCP), where she also served as an adjunct instructor and internship supervisor. Previously, she worked with leadership and service–learning in the UMCP Scholars living–learning program and in residence life at the University of Missouri and the University of Central Missouri. She served as a research team member for the National Study of Living–Learning Programs and Autoethnographic Research Group. She has researched and presented on such topics as student learning outcomes, leadership self-efficacy, dimensions of identity development, student engagement in living–learning environments, and the motives and experiences of faculty members involved with living–learning programs.

Jennifer Wells is the director of assessment in the Office of Institutional Effectiveness and an assistant professor of higher education in the Department of First-Year and Transition Studies at Kennesaw State University. In her assessment role, she works cooperatively with staff, faculty, administrators, and the Office of Institutional Effectiveness to advance the university's continuous improvement initiative. She was previously the director of planning and assessment in student affairs. She earned her PhD in college student affairs administration from the University of Georgia; her dissertation focused on the psychosocial development of students with the Broader Autism Phenotype. She is editor of the *CAS Professional Standards for Higher Education* (9th edition).

Index

Figures and tables are indicated by "f" and "t" following the page number.

A

Academic advising divisions, xiii, 61–75
  action plan development, 65, 74–75
  challenges in, 70–72
  example of standards use, 64–67, 67f
  initial considerations for, 63–64
  institutional background and, 62
  lessons from, 72–74
  recommendations for, 68–72
Access, residence life reviews and, 98
Accountability in higher education
  accreditation and, 2–3, 28, 36
  student affairs assessment and, 50
  student learning outcomes and, 18, 22
Accreditation
  accountability and, 2–3, 28, 36
  preparing for, 78–79
  reaffirming, xiii, 36, 63–64, 135
  from SACS, 38
  standards for, 4, 10, 28
  student services data and, 123
Achieving the Dream: Community
  Colleges Count, 62
ACPA (American College Personnel
  Association), 4, 35
Action plans
  for academic advising divisions,
    65, 74–75
  example of, 145–149
  for housing and residence life, 103
  for LGBTQ services, 115
  low ratings and, 31
  for multicampus institutions, 84–85
  overview, 13–15
  productivity of CAS reviews and, 36
  for regional institutions, 39, 44

Advocacy, LGBTQ services and, 110–113
Alcohol and Other Drug Programs
  (AODP) SAG, 58–59
Alumni associations, 122
American College Personnel
  Association (ACPA), 4, 35
Annual funds, 122
Annual procedures, 46
Annual reports and summaries,
  54, 54f, 128, 159–161
Arkansas State University–Beebe
  (ASU–Beebe), 77–78. *See also*
  Multicampus institutions
Assessment. *See* Self-assessments
  and program reviews
Assessment culture. *See*
  Culture of assessment
Assessment cycles. *See* Cycles of assessment
Assessment tracking systems, 85
Assistant vice presidents for student affairs
  (AVPs), 29–30, 33, 128, 141–142
Association of American Colleges
  & Universities, 109
Astin, A. W., 91–92

B

Baylor University (BU). *See*
  Housing and residence life
Behavior
  ethics and, 97–98
  student learning outcomes and, 23
Benchmarks
  CAS professional standards as, 10–11
  cycles of assessment and, 44
  example of, 111–112
  housing and residence halls and, 91

institutional advocacy and, 110–113
lessons from, 112–113
for student learning outcomes, 109
surveys for, 91, 99
training on, 41–42
Bias, 71, 82
Bloom, B. S., 23
Board of Directors of CAS, 6, 112
Bullard, Cora, 42
Buy-in
achieving, 134–135
of colleagues, 11
of leaders, 93
prior CAS knowledge and, 51
resistance to assessment and, 39
of staff, 31, 80
of stakeholders, 11, 134, 137–138

C

CACREP (Council for the Accreditation
of Counseling and Related
Educational Programs), 4
Candida, Robert, 41
Career services, 43, 56, 125, 128–129
CAS. *See* Council for the Advancement
of Standards in Higher Education
CAS professional standards, xi, 1–16
accountability and, 2–3
cross-functional, 119–131. *See also*
Cross-functional standards
for divisions, 27–36. *See also*
Divisionwide approach
to standards
employing, 15–16
examples and lessons from use, 133–139
flexibility of, 123–124,
129–130, 134, 136
focus of, 5, 36
functional areas of. *See* Functional
area standards
General Standards, 8–9. *See also*
General Standards of CAS
history of, 1, 3–6, 133
LGBT Programs and Services standards
and guidelines of, 108
philosophy of, 6–8, 39–40, 135

purpose of, xiv–xv
questions for consideration, 138–139
Self-Assessment Guides. *See* Self-
Assessment Guides
for self-assessments, 11–15. *See also* Self-
assessments and program reviews
self-regulation and, 10–11
Student Leadership Programs
section of, 125–126
Student learning and development
domains and dimensions of, 16,
20–21, 53–56, 107–110, 163
for student learning outcomes, 17–25.
See also Student learning and
development outcomes
Transfer Student Programs
and Services section of, 125
*CAS Professional Standards for Higher
Education* (CAS), xi, 1–2, 5, 50
*CAS Review Executive Summary and
Action Plan*, 32, 34, 145–149
Chair of review teams, 44–46, 65, 82
Challenges in self-assessment
for academic advising divisions, 70–72
cross-functional standards and, 126–127
for divisionwide use of standards, 32
for housing and residence life
divisions, 103
for LGBTQ services, 108–109
for multicampus institutions, 85–86
for student affairs divisions, 32
for teams for self-assessments, 116
Change model (Prochaska
& DiClementi), 40
Change resulting from self-
assessments. *See* Action plans
Class gifts, 122
Clearinghouses, 73, 121
Collaboration
accountability and, 3
cross-functional, 3, 50–51, 59–60
with faculty members, 3, 31,
44, 66, 80, 83
General Standards and, 9
housing and residence life
reviews and, 98
of professional organizations, 4–5

for program review, 44–45, 66
with staff, 11, 31, 80
student affairs divisions and, 59–60
for student learning outcomes, 24
Colleagues. *See also* Faculty members; Staff
buy-in from, 11
program review and, 44–45
student learning outcomes and, 24
Colleges. *See* Institutions
Community colleges, 61. *See also*
Academic advising divisions
Completion rates of students, 2, 19
Conditions for student
learning outcomes, 23
Conferences for training, 54–55
Confidentiality, 32, 97–98
Consolidations of schools, 52–53
Consortium of Higher Education LGBT
Resource Professionals, 105, 112
Continuous improvement model, 64–65,
136–138. *See also* Cycles of assessment
Coordinators of self-assessments,
30–31, 33, 93, 141–143
Corrective actions, 13–14, 143
COSPA (Council of Student Personnel
Associations in Higher Education), 4
Council for the Accreditation of
Counseling and Related Educational
Programs (CACREP), 4
Council for the Advancement of Standards
in Higher Education (CAS)
Board of Directors, 6, 112
*CAS Professional Standards for Higher
Education*, xi, 1–2, 5, 50
*CAS Review Executive Summary and
Action Plan*, 32, 34, 145–149
General Standards. *See* General
Standards of CAS
history of, 1, 3–6, 133
philosophy of, 6–8, 39–40, 135
professional standards, 1–16. *See also*
CAS professional standards
Self-Assessment Guides. *See* Self-
Assessment Guides
Council of Student Personnel
Associations in Higher
Education (COSPA), 4

Counseling. *See* Academic advising
divisions; Career services
Crain, Léna Kavaliauskas, xiv, 119
Credibility of self-assessments, 12, 35–36
Criterion measures
challenges of, 70–72
documents based on, 70
evidence and, 84
ratings based on, 58, 115, 115*f*, 142
Cross-functional standards, xiv, 119–131
approach to self-assessment
and, 122–124
campus and departmental
context, 120–122
challenges in, 126–127
design of self-assessment and, 124–126
practice recommendations for, 129–130
reporting for, 127–129
Cross-functional training, 39, 44–45
Culture
institutional, 38, 136
multiculturalism and, 7, 61, 105–106
philosophy of CAS and, 7
student ethnicity and, 61
Culture of assessment
cross-functional standards and, 126
leadership for, 33
at multicampus institutions, 83–84
at regional institutions, 38, 43
strategies for, xiv
for student affairs divisions, xii, 50
Cummings, Robin, 37
Cycles of assessment
for academic advising, 64–68, 67*t*, 71–72
alterations to, 85
for continuous improvement, 136–138
cross-functional training for, 44, 46–47
external reviews and, 44, 47
for multicampus institutions, 80, 81*f*, 84
recommendations for, 71–72
for student affairs, 123
timeline for, 143–144

D

Data collection. *See also* Evidence
for accreditation, 123

clearinghouses for, 73, 121
multicampus institutions and, 71–72
reaffirmation of accreditation and, 64
self-assessment design and, 124
worksheets for, 39
Deadlines, 32. *See also* Cycles
of assessment; Timelines
for self-assessments
Dean, Laura A., ix
Dean, Shannon R., xii, 17
Department of Education, 62
Departments
annual summaries of, 159–161
cross-functional standards and, 120–122
representatives of, 29, 33, 123
reviews of, 11–15, 34–35, 38
DiClementi, Carlo, 40
Dining services, 86
Diversity. *See also* LGBTQ services
academic advising and, 69
community colleges and, 61
housing and residence life
reviews and, 98
multicampus institutions and, 78
multiculturalism and, 7, 61, 105–106
philosophy of CAS and, 7
Divisionwide approach to
standards, xii, 27–36
academic advising divisions and,
61–75. *See also* Academic
advising divisions
challenges for, 32
leadership and, 27–28
recommendations for, 29–32
at regional institutions, 37–48. *See
also* Regional institutions
reporting process for, 34–35
small and medium institutions
and, 33–34
student affairs divisions and, 49–60. *See
also* Student affairs divisions
VPSA perspective and, 33, 35–36
Documentation. *See* Data
collection; Evidence
Duncan, A., 2

E

Educational access, 2
Educational Benchmarking,
Inc. (EBI), 91, 99
Educational events for seniors, 122
Employment, 32, 40
Enrollment rates of students, 18, 61, 78
Equity, residence life reviews and, 98
Ethics, 7, 97–98
Ethnicity, 61, 98. *See also* Diversity
Evidence. *See also* Culture of assessment
archival and coding of, 72–73
clearinghouses for, 73, 121
criterion measures and, 84
feedback on, 84–85
functional areas and, 65–67
gathering, 70–73, 95, 114–115,
123, 141–142
from human resources, 97, 99
lack of, 100
multicampus institutions and, 71–72
overview, 12–13
for reaffirmation of accreditation, 64
self-assessment design and, 124
of student learning, 2–3, 19
from student services for
accreditation, 123
tracking systems for, 85
transparency and, 137–138
worksheets for, 39
Evidence-based practice, 24
Executive summaries
authors of, 142
cross-functional standards and, 127–129
disseminating, 142
editing, 143
multicampus institutions and, 84
purpose of, 14–15, 36
template for, 32, 34–35, 145–149
External reviews
changes based on, 42
cycles of assessment and, 44, 47
functional area knowledge and, 71, 74
recommendations for, 83
self-assessment vs., 10
to validate assessment use, 139

F

Facilities uses, 99, 127
Faculty members
    change instigation of, 102
    collaboration with, 3, 31, 44, 66, 80, 83
    partner programs with, 101
    on review teams, 83
Failure of assessments, 79, 92
Fatigue, self-assessment, 73
Feedback
    action-oriented, 43
    from leadership teams, 84–85
    in pilot trainings, 43–44
    from stakeholders, 80
    on student learning outcome
        development, 24
    surveys for, 39, 55
Finances
    accountability for, 19
    grants, 62
    housing and residence life
        reviews and, 99–101
    philanthropic events, 122
    for self-assessments, 32
    senior-year programs and, 122
Fink, D., 23
First-time-in-college (FTIC)
    students, 69–70, 74
Focus groups for evidence, 19
Fraternities and sororities, 43, 59–60
Functional area standards
    academic advising divisions and, 65–66
    consolidation of schools and, 52–53
    cross-functional standards and, 119–131.
        See also Cross-functional standards
    external reviewers for, 71, 74
    interdisciplinary standards, 129–130
    silos in, 8–9
    student affairs divisions and, 57–58
    teams' knowledge of, 12, 14
Fundraising, 122

G

Garrett, Deborah, xiii, 77, 78–79, 83
Gender services, 57. *See also*
    LGBTQ services

General Standards of CAS
    employing, 15–16
    flexibility of, 123–124, 129–130, 136
    limitations of, 124–125
    modifying, 15
    overview, 8–9
    self-assessment design and, 124–126
    student learning outcomes and,
        20–21, 53–54, 55*f*
    subsections of, 8, 20–21, 53, 58–59
    training in, 94, 135
General use of CAS standards. *See*
    Divisionwide approach to standards
Global Understanding and Social Justice
    Living–Learning Communities, 96
Goals and objectives. *See also*
    Strategic planning
    of institutions, 46
    mission statements of institutions,
        42, 46, 50–51, 95, 151–154
    in program review, 41–42
    strategic, 51–52, 51*f*
    student learning outcomes vs., 19–20
    worksheets for, 41, 152,
        155–157, 159–161
Graduate assistants, 114–115, 121
Graduate interns, 114–116
Grants, 62
Greek life, 43, 59–60
Green sheets (worksheets for
    goals), 41, 46, 159–161
Gulley, Needham Yancey, xiv, 133

H

Hardin-Simmons University (HSU).
    See Housing and residence life
Higher education institutions.
    See Institutions
Housing and residence life, xiii, 89–104
    assessment plans for, 99–100
    challenges of assessments, 103
    change, implementing, 102–104
    diversity, equity, and access in, 98
    ethics and, 97–98
    facilities and equipment for, 99
    financing for, 99–101

human resources and, 97
internal and external relations
        and, 98–99
law, policy, and governance and, 98
LGBTQ services and, 112
mission statements and, 95
multicampus institutions and, 78, 83
organization and leadership for, 96–97
program for, 95–96
purpose of, 90–92
ratings for, 100–102
teams for assessment of, 92–94
technology for, 99
Humanitarianism and civic engagement
        domain of CAS, 109–110
Human resources, 7, 69, 97,
        99, 101. *See also* Staff

I

I-E-O model (inputs, environment,
        and outputs), 91–92
Institutional advocacy, 110–113
Institutions
        accountability in, 2–3
        culture of, 136
        enrollment rates, 18
        finances of. *See* Finances
        large. *See* Cross-functional standards
        merging of, 52–53
        mission and vision statements of, 42,
                46, 50–51, 95, 151–154
        multicampus, 77–88. *See also*
                Multicampus institutions
        philosophy of CAS and, 7
        public scrutiny of, 1, 18
        small, 33–35, 89–104. *See also*
                Housing and residence life
        student affairs, 49–60. *See also*
                Student affairs divisions
Interdisciplinary standards, 129–130
Internal decisions, 30–31, 127–128
Internal reviews. *See* Self-assessments
        and program reviews
Interns, 114–116
Interviews for evidence, 19

J

Job-searches. *See* Career services
Jones, John R., III, xii, 37

K

Keeling, R. P., 109
Kennesaw State University (KSU), 49–50.
        See also Student affairs divisions

L

Lange, Alex C., xiii, 105
Large institutions. *See* Cross-functional
        standards; LGBTQ services
Law, residence life reviews and, 98
Leaders
        action plan summaries for, 14–15
        buy-in for assessment, 93
        chairs for self-assessment teams,
                12, 44–45, 65, 82
        coordinators of self-assessments,
                30–31, 33, 93, 141–143
        housing and residence life
                reviews and, 96–97
        philosophy of CAS and, 7
        prior experience of, 86
        priorities of, 27–28
        recommendations for, 33, 135–136
        student learning outcomes and, 37–38
        students as, 55–56, 107
        of units under review, 12
LEAP (Liberal Education and
        America's Promise), 109
Learning outcomes. *See* Student learning
        and development outcomes
Learning Reconsidered (Keeling), 109
LGBT Programs and Services standards
        and guidelines of CAS (2009), 108
LGBTQ (lesbian, gay, bisexual, trans,
        and queer) services, xiii, 105–117
        benchmarking and, 110–113
        CAS standards and guidelines for, 108
        challenges of, 108–109
        lessons from, 109–110
        Self-Assessment Guide use and, 113–117

student learning outcomes and, 106–110

Liberal Education and America's Promise (LEAP), 109

Living–learning programs, 96, 100–102

Longwood University, 27, 145–149. *See also* Divisionwide approach to standards

Lumbee tribe members, 37–38

M

Mable, Phyllis, 27

Mann, R., 90

Matthews, D., 2

Mayes, David, xiii, 77

McKenzie, Onie, xii, 27, 28

Measurability of student learning outcomes, 20, 22–24

Merging of schools, 52–53

Michigan State University (MSU), 107, 114

Mid-sized institutions, 33–34. *See also* Regional institutions

Minorities. *See* Diversity; LGBTQ services

Mission and vision statements of institutions, 42, 46, 50–51, 95, 151–154

Monthly reports for self-assessments, 46

Multicampus institutions, xiii, 77–88. *See also* Academic advising divisions
action plans for, 84–85
ASU-Beebe overview, 77–78
challenges for, 85–86
cycles of assessment for, 80, 81*f*, 84
data collection for, 72–73
lessons from, 87
program design for, 79–80
review teams for, 82–84
student learning outcomes and, 81–82

Multiculturalism, 7, 61, 105–106

Multifunctional standards. *See* Cross-functional standards

N

National Association of Student Personnel Administrators (NASPA), 4, 35

National Survey of Student Engagement, 91

Native Americans, 37–38

Negative consequences of self-assessments, 31, 79, 92, 138

Nelson, Joretta, 90

O

Objectives. *See* Goals and objectives

Operational effectiveness, 51

Operational working groups (OWG), 52

Outcome planning, 151–154

P

Part-time students, 61

Pennington, H., 1

Performance evaluations, 39–40

Philanthropic events, 122

Philosophy of CAS, 6–7, 39–40, 135

Pierson, Tim James, xii, 27

Pilot training review, 43–44

Policy, housing and residence life reviews and, 98

Positive outlook, 39, 42

Practical competence, 56

Presentations on self-assessments, 14–15, 34, 73, 84

Presidents, 28

Priorities. *See* Goals and objectives

Privacy, 32, 97–98

Private institutions. *See* Housing and residence life

Prochaska, James, 40

Professional associations, ix, 3–6, 18

Professional Competencies for Student Affairs Educators (ACPA & NASPA), 35

Professional development, ix, 87, 96

Professional standards. *See* CAS professional standards

Program development, xiii, 18, 21–22, 128

Program reviews. *See* Self-assessments and program reviews

Project SSStrong, 62

R

Race, 61, 98. *See also* Diversity
Raleigh, Mary-Jeanne, xii, 37
Ratings for self-assessments
    benefits of, 87
    bias in, 71, 82
    divisionwide approach to
        standards and, 30–32
    evidence for, 84
    housing and residence life reviews
        and, 100–102
    LGBTQ services and, 115, 115*t*
    overview, 13
Readiness for program review,
    39–41, 78–79
Reaffirmation of accreditation,
    xiii, 36, 63–64, 135
Redundancy in self-assessments, 71
*Reference Guide for Student Success
    and Gender Identity and
    Expression* (GIE), 111–112
Regional institutions, xii, 37–48
    academic advising and, 61–75. *See also*
        Academic advising divisions
    beginning assessments, 38–39
    cross-functional training at, 44–45
    cycles of assessment at, 46–47
    forms and elements for, 45–46
    readiness for assessment, 39–41
    resistance to assessment, 39
    training reviews at, 43–44
    training workshops at, 40–43
Reports for self-assessments. *See*
    Executive summaries
Research institutions. *See* LGBTQ services
Residence life. *See* Housing
    and residence life
Resident assistants (RAs), 98
Resistance to self-assessments,
    39, 138. *See also* Buy-in
Resources. *See also* Finances
    development objectives for, 46
    limitations on, 32, 126, 139
    presidents use of, 28
Results of program reviews.
    See Action plans

Retention of students, 69–70
Retreats for training, 42, 80, 81–82
Review chairs, 12, 44–46, 65, 82
Review teams. *See* Teams for
    self-assessments
Rodriguez, Adrian, xiii, 61
Roles for self-assessment, 31, 141–144
Rozeboom, Dave, xiii, 89
Rubrics, 19, 42
Rural institutions, 35

S

SAALOG (Student Affairs
    Assessment and Learning
    Outcomes Group), 123, 128
SACS (Southern Association of Colleges
    and Schools), 38, 62–64, 70
Safety assessments, 98–99
Schedules for self-assessments. *See*
    Cycles of assessment; Timelines
    for self-assessments
Schools. *See* Institutions
Schulze, Louann, xiii, 61
Self-Assessment Guides (SAGs)
    for academic advising, 68–69
    Alcohol and Other Drug
        Programs, 58–59
    data collection and, 124
    example of, 114–115, 115*t*
    LGBTQ services and, 113–117
    recommendations for use, 29–31
    for student affairs divisions, 58–60
    training for, 66
    vague terms in, 127
Self-assessments and program reviews
    of academic advising divisions,
        61–75. *See also* Academic
        advising divisions
    action plans resulting from, 13–14.
        See also Action plans
    challenges in. *See* Challenges
        in self-assessment
    credibility of, 12, 35–36
    culture of assessment. *See* Culture
        of assessment
    customizing, 29–30

cycles of assessment. *See* Cycles
     of assessment
designing, 124–126
divisionwide, 27–36. *See also*
     Divisionwide approach
     to standards
evidence for, 12–13. *See also* Evidence
example of, 145–149
failure of, 79, 92
fatigue from, 73
of housing and residence life,
     79–104. *See also* Housing
     and residence life
leaders of. *See* Leaders
of LGBTQ services, 105–117. *See
     also* LGBTQ services
at multicampus institutions, 77–88. *See
     also* Multicampus institutions
overview, 1–16. *See also* CAS
     professional standards
planning, 11
presentations on, 14–15, 34, 73, 84
ratings for, 13. *See also* Ratings
     for self-assessments
readiness for, 39–41, 78–79
redundancies in, 71
at regional institutions, 37–48. *See
     also* Regional institutions
resistance to, 39, 138. *See also* Buy-in
roles for, 31, 141–144
of student affairs divisions, 49–60. *See
     also* Student affairs divisions
summarizing, 14–15. *See also*
     Executive summaries
teams for, 12. *See also* Teams
     for self-assessments
technology for, 72–73, 85, 99, 141
timelines for, 114–116, 124, 126–127,
     143–144, 159–161
tools for. *See* Tools and resources
training for. *See* Training for
     self-assessments
VPSA role, 142
Self-regulation, 10–11, 53
Senior Council, 121, 125–126
Senior experience coordinator, 121–122
Senior leadership, 93

Senior-year programs, 119–120. *See
     also* Cross-functional standards
Severy, Michael, 47
Sexuality programs, 57. *See
     also* LGBTQ services
Sexual Violence–Related
     Programs and Services, 57
Sharp, Marybeth Drechsler, xi, 1
Siloes of information, 8–9
Skepticism, 138
SLDOs. *See* Student learning and
     development outcomes
Small institutions, 33–35. *See also*
     Housing and residence life;
     Multicampus institutions
Social events for seniors, 122
Soliday, J., 90
Southern Association of Colleges and
     Schools (SACS), 38, 62–64, 70
Southern Polytechnic State
     University, 49–50, 52
Staff
     background knowledge of, 109
     collaboration with, 11, 31, 80
     cycles of assessment and, 72–73
     dedicated to self-assessment, 135–136
     limitations on, 32
     students as, 33–34, 121, 126–127
     training. *See* Training for
          self-assessments
Stakeholders
     action plan summaries for, 14–15
     buy-in from, 11, 134, 137–138
     feedback from, 80
     review of self-assessment
          materials, 114–115
     teamwork and, 29, 116
Standards. *See* CAS professional standards
St. Edward's University (SEU). *See*
     Housing and residence life
Strategic planning
     academic advising and, 62–64
     housing and residence life
          reviews and, 96
     self-assessment as, 38
     student affairs divisions and,
          41–42, 50–52, 51*f*

Student Affairs Assessment and
  Learning Outcomes Group
  (SAALOG), 123, 128
Student affairs divisions, xii, 49–60
  annual summary worksheets
      for, 159–161
  assessment officers for, 49
  challenges for, 32
  consolidation of schools and, 52–53
  functional area standards and, 57–58
  housing and residence life reviews
      and, 89–104. *See also*
      Housing and residence life
  institutional context and, 49–52, 51*f*
  planning and assessment worksheets
      for, 155–157
  Self-Assessment Guides and, 58–60
  student learning outcomes and,
      18–19, 53–56, 54–55*f*
"Student Development Services in Post-
  Secondary Education" (Cooper), 4
Student Leadership Programs
  section of CAS, 125–126
Student learning and development
  domains and dimensions of CAS,
  16, 20–21, 53–56, 107–110, 163
Student learning and development
  outcomes (SLDOs), xii, 17–25
  academic advising divisions and, 66, 69–70
  accountability for, 2–3
  CAS self-studies and, 27
  defined, 20
  developing, 21–22, 109–110
  directors' and assistant vice
      chancellors' focus on, 39
  General Standards and, 20–21,
      53–54, 55*f*
  housing and residence halls
      reviews and, 91, 95–96
  importance of, 18–19
  learning objectives vs., 19–20
  LGBTQ services and, 106–110
  monthly reports on, 46
  for multicampus institutions, 81–82
  program review and, 41–43
  student affairs divisions and,
      50–51, 53–56, 54–55*f*

worksheets for outcome
      planning, 151–154
  writing, 20–24
Students
  academic advising requirements
      for, 69–70
  completion rates of, 2, 19
  diversity of, 78
  enrollment rates of, 18, 61, 78
  first-time-in-college (FTIC), 69–70, 74
  Greek life and, 43, 59–60
  housing and residence halls reviews
      and, 89–104. *See also*
      Housing and residence life
  as interns, 114–116
  leadership plans for, 55–56, 107
  philosophy of CAS and, 6–7
  retention of, 69–70
  senior-year programs for, 119–120. *See
      also* Cross-functional standards
  as staff, 33–34, 121, 126–127
Study spaces, 99
*Suggested Best Practices for Supporting
  Trans* Students* (Consortium
  of Higher Education LGBT
  Resource Professionals), 112
Summaries of self-assessments.
  See Executive summaries
Summer assessments, 114–115, 126
Summer retreats, 42
Surveys
  for benchmarking, 91, 99
  for evidence collection, 19, 142
  on program review, 39
  on training, 55
Surviving to Thriving (Soliday & Mann), 90
Sustainability practices, 96–97

T

Tarrant County College District, 62. *See
  also* Academic advising divisions
Teams for self-assessments
  chair of, 12, 44–45, 65, 82
  challenges for, 116
  committees for oversight and
      training, 45–46

divisionwide use of standards
    and, 29–33
faculty members and, 83
functional area knowledge of, 12, 14, 66
graduate assistants and, 114–115
of housing and residence life
    reviews, 92–94
of multicampus institutions, 82–84
overview, 12–14
recommendations for, 135–136
role of, 143
stakeholders and, 29, 116
strengths of, 73
training for. *See* Training for
    self-assessments
Technology for self-assessments,
    72–73, 85, 99, 141
Thomas, Bud, 120
Timelines for self-assessments, 114–116,
    124, 126–127, 143–144, 159–161.
    See also Cycles of assessment
Tools and resources
    CAS review executive summary
        and action plan, 145–149
    CAS self-study roles, responsibilities,
        and timeline, 141–144
    department annual summary (green
        sheets), 41, 46, 159–161
    outcome planning resource
        sheet, 151–154
    planning and assessment worksheet
        directions, 155–157
    student learning and development
        domains and dimensions, 16,
        20–21, 53–56, 107–110, 163
Tracking systems for assessment, 85
Training for self-assessments
    for academic advising divisions, 65–67, 67f
    cross-functional, 38, 44–45
    evaluating, 54–55
    in General Standards, 94, 135
    at multicampus institutions, 83–84
    of new staff, 46–47
    orientation meetings, 30, 36, 142
    overview, 12
    pilot training review, 41, 43–44
    at regional institutions, 38–39

retreats for, 42, 80, 81–82
    of review chairs, 46
    topics for, 42–43, 135
    workshops for, 40–43, 83–84, 87
Transfer Student Programs and
    Services section of CAS, 125
Transparency, 137–138
Trust, 138

U

Universal learning focus, 56
Universities. *See* Institutions
University of Maryland, College
    Park (UMCP), 119–120. *See also*
    Cross-functional standards
University of North Carolina–
    Pembroke (UNCP), 37–38. *See
    also* Regional institutions

V

Veterans' counselors, 68, 74
Vice presidents. *See* Divisionwide
    approach to standards
Vice presidents of student affairs
    (VPSAs), 33–36, 142
Vision and mission statements
    of institutions, 42, 46,
    50–51, 95, 151–154
Volunteers, 33–34

W

Wages, 40
Wells, Jennifer, xi, xii, 49
Wheelan, Elgart, 10
Women's and Gender Programs
    and Services, 57
Workforce preparedness, 2
Worksheets
    for data collection, 39
    department annual summaries, 159–161
    directions for planning and
        assessment, 155–157
    for goals (green sheets),
        41–46, 159–161

for outcome planning, 151–154
for planning and assessment, 155–157
for student learning and development,
     16, 20–21, 53–56, 107–110, 163
Workshops for program review,
     40–43, 83–84, 87
Writing
   executive summaries, 142
   standards, 6
   student learning outcomes, 20–24

Y

Year-end reports and summaries, 46, 97.
   See also Annual reports and summaries

Z

Zanville, H., 2